Heaven In My Heart

Heaven In My Heart

Table of Contents

Dedication

For All of You with Seeking Hearts

*May this be one of many ways
you find your God.*

For this is the secret:
Christ lives in you.

Colossians 1:27 (NLT)

Author's Note

This is a devotional book I have written for girls and young women seeking God and His best for their life. If this describes you, I hope you will find these lessons helpful and encouraging. You will need a Bible to complete each lesson. (If you do not have a Bible, I recommend using the website: www.blueletterbible.org) You don't need to complete an entire lesson in one sitting. Do as much as you have time for, giving adequate thought and attention to each Bible verse or passage, question, and insights I share. Doing a small amount each day will be more beneficial than trying to do a whole lesson and rushing through it.

I have left space for you to write your thoughts and answers to the questions in this book, but you may want to keep a journal or notebook handy to record additional thoughts or prayers, and you will need one to use the journaling guide I introduce in the lesson "Listening To God" and for your personal Bible-reading thereafter. It doesn't have to be anything fancy. An old spiral notebook you only used partially or loose paper stapled together is adequate. Another thing you may want to have on hand are 3x5 index cards. Writing out verses you find especially meaningful and reviewing them several times a week or posting them where you will see them every day will keep your thoughts focused on the truths you are learning.

With the love of Jesus,
Melanie

Where Is Heaven?

"Hear from heaven, your dwelling place..."
1 Kings 8:30

Have you ever wondered what Heaven is like? In the Bible we can read about Heaven. Jesus talked about Heaven a lot. But what is it like there? Where is it? How can we get there? And is there such a thing as Heaven In My Heart? If you have no idea what I mean by that, then this devotional book is for you.

Let's start by thinking about what you already know about Heaven, or at least think you know. All of us have different ideas about it, and some things we can know for sure and some we can't. Where do you think Heaven is, and what do you think Heaven is like? Write down anything that comes to mind.

Read the following Bible verses. What do they say about Heaven?

Genesis 1:1

Exodus 20:22

Deuteronomy 10:14

1 Kings 8:30 (Solomon is praying to God in this verse)

Matthew 4:17

In the Bible, the word *heaven* can mean two things. It can mean the physical heavens—the space above and beyond the earth. (The air, the sky, outer space; the place where the sun, moon, and stars are.) And it can also mean the place where God dwells. Many people assume that God is in the heavens and not here on Earth, but what do Psalm 139:7-10 and Jeremiah 23:24 say?

So, if God is everywhere, and Heaven is where God dwells, what does that say about where Heaven is?

What I believe the Bible teaches us is this: Heaven is where God dwells. And God can be anywhere He wants to be. Heaven and Earth cannot contain Him. He is everywhere.

How does that affect your view of God?

What do you think is good about God being everywhere?

Do you think there is anything bad about God being everywhere? If so, what?

One of the things I like about God being everywhere is I know He is always with me. I can talk to Him anytime I want, and He will hear me. Even if I just talk to Him in my thoughts. Solomon asked God to *"Hear from heaven, your dwelling place."* Spend some time talking to God right now about whatever is on your mind and heart. He will hear you. You can "think" a prayer, say one out loud, or write one in the space provided here or in your journal.

Heaven In Our Hearts

"I am in you." John 14:20

In the first lesson we talked about where Heaven is. We learned Heaven is where God dwells and God is everywhere. Today we are going to read about Jesus. The term "Christian" is used of someone who follows Jesus Christ and His teachings. Whether you call yourself a Christian or not, this lesson will help you to understand more about who Jesus is and what Jesus has to say about Heaven.

What do the following verses say about Jesus?

John 6:38 (Jesus is speaking)

Mark 16:19

John 14:1-3 and 16-20 (Jesus is speaking)

John 10:30 (God is sometimes called the Father)

Galatians 4:6 (Jesus is sometimes called the Son)

Revelation 3:20 (Jesus is speaking)

While Jesus was on Earth, He claimed to be one with God. He was God who came from Heaven (a place we can't see) to where we could see Him. And He came looking like a regular man. He wasn't a spirit or a ghost, but a real-live person.

The Bible tells us Jesus was crucified, an ancient way of putting criminals to death. He hadn't done anything wrong, but He was killed anyway. He died willingly as a way of showing His love and mercy for everyone. He died, but He came back to life. God raised Him from the dead to show His power over death. After this, Jesus went to Heaven. But remember, Heaven is not a far-off place. We cannot see Jesus, but He is still everywhere—all around us. And the place He wants to be is *in us*. He can do that because He is God, and God is Spirit.

Asking Jesus into your life (or heart) isn't just about going to Heaven when you die. It's about entering Heaven now. Entering the Kingdom of Heaven. It isn't out-there somewhere; it can be inside of you! In your mind and heart and actions. At some point in your life, you may have said a prayer like the one below, or maybe you haven't. Prayer is simply expressing your heart to God. If you agree with the words I have written, you can say the same thing to God with your voice, in your thoughts, or by writing these or similar words in a journal.

Jesus, I believe you died for me so I can be forgiven of all the wrong things I have done. I believe you rose from the dead and have gone to Heaven so I can be a part of your Kingdom and have you inside of me. I believe you love me. Please change me from the inside out. Help me to know you, believe you, obey you, and trust you. Please make me all you

*want me to be and bless me with all of the wonderful things
you have for me. Amen.*

If you have prayed a similar prayer in the past or did so for the first
time today, take some time to be silent before God and listen.
What do you hear Jesus saying to you?

Look back at the verses written at the beginning (under the title) of
the two lessons we've done so far. Write the words on the
following blank page, on index cards, or in your journal or
notebook. Review these verses often and try to add one verse that
"speaks" to you from each lesson. You may want to keep them
where you can review them each time you do this study, post them
somewhere you will see them often, or carry them with you
wherever you go.

The Kingdom Of Heaven

"The kingdom of heaven is near."
Matthew 4:17

Today we are going to look more at why God (Jesus) wants to be in our hearts, and why we would want Him there. Keep in mind that when you read about the Father, the Son, Jesus Christ, or the Spirit, it's all talking about God. God has many different names and functions in many different ways, but it's all the same God. The Creator of the heavens and the earth. The God who made you.

What does Isaiah 66:1 say about Heaven?

Jesus often talked about the Kingdom of Heaven (or Kingdom of God). What comes to mind when you think about a kingdom? (Use a dictionary if you need to.)

Who is in charge of a kingdom?

A kingdom is basically anyplace where there is some organized form of government where someone is in charge (usually a king or queen), and everyone who lives in that country or region is expected to obey the laws of that kingdom.

In our world there are good kingdoms and bad kingdoms. Usually a good kingdom has a good ruler and a bad kingdom has a bad ruler. When Jesus speaks of the Kingdom of Heaven, He's talking about a place where God is leading and making the rules. According to Psalm 34:8, is God a good king or a bad king?

In what ways have you seen God's goodness?

What does Jesus say about the Kingdom of Heaven in the following verses?

Matthew 4:17

Matthew 6:33

Matthew 13:44-46

Just like Heaven, the Kingdom of Heaven is not a far-off place. It is close. To seek the Kingdom of God is to know Him and allow Him to care for us by obeying Him and trusting Him. But we have a choice: We can be in charge of our own lives and not let God rule us at all; we can be in charge some of the time and let God have His way sometimes; or we can give up all control and let God reign in our hearts all of the time, doing what He says and trusting Him to take care of us always. Of these choices, what would you say is true for you currently?

(Don't be discouraged if you aren't able to give the answer you would like to give. The purpose of this devotional-study is to help you grow in your relationship with God.)

Choose one of the verses from today to add to your note card collection (or wherever you are writing them), review them all, and think about how they relate to the response you gave above.

Talk to God about where you are now and where you want to be.

Treasure Of Heaven

*"The kingdom of heaven is like treasure
hidden in a field...
like a merchant looking for fine pearls."
Matthew 13:44-45*

In the previous lesson we talked about what the Kingdom of Heaven is. Review your answers to recall the major points we talked about. Having those thoughts fresh in your mind will help you grasp what you read today.

Read Matthew 13:44-46

Jesus compares the Kingdom of Heaven to a treasure that someone finds and then gives up everything else to have that one treasure. Why is the Kingdom of Heaven (seeking God, knowing Him, trusting Him) so valuable according to the following verses? (Some of these you may want to write on index cards to review later or post where you will see them often.)

Psalm 34:4-7

Psalm 34:8-10

John 6:47-51 (Jesus is speaking)

1 John 4:15-16

Do you know and rely on the love God has for you? Are you living in His love? Do you believe in His goodness? This is the treasure worth finding. Sometimes we think of the Kingdom of God as something we must earn the right to. But there's nothing to earn. It's about entering it and receiving all that God has for you. Primarily His love.

On a scale from one to ten, ten being highest, how confident are you that God loves you? How much of His love are you receiving? A little, some, or all that He has to give you?

1—2—3—4—5—6—7—8—9—10

My prayer for you is that this number will increase as you do the lessons in this book. Even if you're at a ten now, there's always more of His love to take in as you know Him more and grow closer to Him. And that's really what it's all about: Learning to delight in your God because He loves you and His love is always enough. It will lead the way to discovering the plans God has for you. It can get you through the difficult days. It will help you feel better about yourself and how valuable you are to God and others. And it will give you a one-way ticket into all of the wonderful blessings He has waiting for you.

Write the following phrase at least five times:

God Loves Me

Seeking and Seeing

"Seek first his kingdom..." Matthew 6:33

In Matthew 6:33 Jesus tells us that we should *"Seek first his kingdom and his righteousness, and all these things will be given to you as well."* What this basically means is that seeking God and the life He has for you is the most important thing you can do. It is life-changing. It matters. It is for your own good, not just something you should do because your parents, your youth pastor, or I say so. And no one can force you to do it, not even God. Seeking God is a choice for you to make for yourself.

Read Jeremiah 29:11-13

What does God say in verse 11?

What do you think it means to seek God with all of your heart?

You can learn a lot about God by going to church and listening to others teach about Him. I hope you will learn a lot by doing this devotional book and reading some of the stories God has given me. But my ultimate hope is that you will learn to hear God and learn from God Himself. Sometimes He may speak to you through teachers or books you read. But the most thrilling way to learn about Him is to have Him teach you directly. This is one of the reasons He wants to be inside of you—within your heart and mind so He can teach you about Himself.

What are some practical, everyday ways you can seek God?

How many of the above are you currently doing? How often?

There's a difference between knowing *about* Jesus and *knowing* Him. There's a difference between believing *in* Jesus and *believing* Him. Knowing *about* Jesus and believing *in* Jesus—you likely already do. But do you *know* Him, like the way you know a really close friend or family member? Do you *believe* Him? When He says, 'I know the plans I have for you, and they are good plans!', do you believe Him? When He says, 'Pray to me and I will listen. Seek Me and you will find Me.', do you believe Him?

There are many ways to seek God, and I believe some ways may work for one person but may not work for another. God wants you to enjoy Him, and if you are getting to know God in an enjoyable way for you, then that's a good way for you. Don't force yourself to do things to seek God, learn about Him, worship Him, or serve Him in ways you don't like. I am a shy and quiet person. My husband is loud and connects easily with anybody. We are very different, and we worship, serve, and learn about God in different ways. That's okay. You don't have to be like someone else. All God wants is for you to be yourself—after all, that is the way He made you!

But I would like to point out two ways that are very important if you want to seek God with all of your heart. One of them is reading the Bible. If you're doing this study, then you're on the right track there, and I will always try to point you to what God has to say about things, not just give my own opinion. Reading the Bible for yourself is important because it helps you to listen to God, not just hear what others say about Him. And listening to God is an important part of knowing Him by hearing what He has to say *to you*. He has plans for you that aren't like plans He has for anyone else. And only He can show you.

I would suggest that you alternate days between doing this devotional book and reading the Bible on your own. Tomorrow's lesson will show you how to go about that. Pick a place in the Bible to start reading and do that for one or two days, and then come back to the next lesson in this devotional book, and so on.

Another way of seeking God is to be looking for Him in your everyday life. If you're having a good day, thank Him for all the good things and learn to recognize that those things come from Him and He wants to bless you. Get in the habit of seeing your life as a gift from God and thank Him regularly for the ways He has blessed you.

And if you're having a bad day or going through a difficult time, learn to go to Him and ask for help. He is there, and He has a purpose for whatever you're going through. Don't ignore your problems or try to handle them yourself. Go to Him and say, 'This is really hard, God, and I need help! Show me what to do; Give me strength; Help me to love that person even though they hurt me; Help me to see You in this and to learn whatever You're trying to teach me.'

Start right now. Write out a prayer to God on the following page or in your journal, thanking Him for the good things, and asking for His help with the bad. Be honest with Him about how you feel and what you need. He is there with you, and He is listening.

Jesus, thank you for...

Jesus, I really need help with...

Listening To God

"Listen, listen to me, and eat what is good,
and your soul will delight in the richest of fare."
Isaiah 55:2

Today is all about you and God. God speaking, and you listening. As I mentioned in the previous lesson, I encourage you to begin reading a specific book in the Bible and read on your own for one or two days and then do the next lesson in this book, and so on. Today I have lined out a specific way of reading the Bible and getting the most out of it. You can use the available space on the following pages to write about what you read today, but in future days you will need a notebook or journal to record your thoughts, or you may make copies of the journaling guide in the back of the book. In the future you may want to modify it or eliminate it altogether as you find what works best for you. But use this guide for now to help focus your thoughts and prayers. Some of the questions may not apply to everything you read, so just answer the ones that do.

If you don't know where to read, some good books to start with are Genesis, Psalms, any of the four gospels (Matthew, Mark, Luke, or John), Galatians, Ephesians, Philippians, Colossians, or 1 John. You can read one or two verses at a time or a whole chapter and focus on what stands out to you most. Before you begin, take some time to pray and see if God is leading you to a specific place to start, and then follow this journaling format:

Date_____
Today I read_____

What does it say? (Write out the exact words of one or two verses, or briefly summarize what is going on.)

What does this mean in my own words? (Restate the verse or passage as if you are telling someone else.)

How can this specifically apply to my life?

What changes do I need to make because of what it says?

How can this be an encouragement to me?

What do I hear God saying to me?

What is my response to Him?

Knowing His Love

"For God so loved the world..."
John 3:16

Let's start today by taking a little quiz. Respond to the following questions as honestly as you can. Resist the temptation to write the answer you think you should rather than how you honestly *feel*. For each question choose one of these responses:

None, A Little, Some, A Lot, Very much!

How much does God love me right now?

How much will God love me a year from now?

How much does God love me when I believe in Him?

How much does God love me when I doubt Him?

How much does God love me when I go to church, read my Bible, and pray?

How much does God love me when I ignore Him?

How much does God love me when I do good things?

How much does God love me when I do wrong things (sin)?

Read Psalm 107:1; Psalm 108:4; and Romans 8:38-39. (Also write at least one of these on an index card)

What do these verses tell you about God's love?

Based on these verses, what should the answer to every question in the quiz be?

If you gave any response other than *very much* (which is fine, I told you to be honest about how you feel), why do you think you don't always believe God loves you as much as He possibly can all the time?

If God loves us all the time, no matter what, then why should we bother to believe in Him, go to church, read the Bible, pray, and do the right things?

If you have ever done something wrong or gone weeks without spending any time learning about God or seeking Him, does that make you feel far away from Him? And how do you feel when you are doing the right things, going to church, and spending time with God by reading the Bible and praying? God feels closer when you're constantly being reminded of His love, right? You see, God doesn't want us to believe in Him, do the right things, and spend time learning about Him so He can love us more, He already loves us so much we can't even comprehend it!

He wants us to do these things so we will be reminded of His love and experience it to its fullest degree. The Bible says, *"For God so loved the world..."* not, 'God so loved the world because they were good.' Believe in His love. Embrace it as much as you can. It's free to whoever wants it.

What things can you do to experience God's love more?

Memorize Psalm 107:1

Knowing God

"I have made you known to them..."
John 17:26

Let's say you have a family member who lives far away whom you have never met. Maybe it's a cousin whose parents moved to another country before she was born and they've never visited. You know about her. You know she exists. Maybe you've seen pictures. But you don't really know her.

One day you decide, 'I want to get to know her and for her to know me.' What things would you do to make that happen?

Whatever you wrote down, they probably involve things you would do directly to contact her like writing letters, email, or phone calls. You wouldn't have your friends write or call her and then tell you what she said. If you had the money to go visit her, you would go yourself, not send your sister in your place. And why? Because the best way to get to know someone is through personal contact.

When Jesus came to Earth, He was doing the same thing. He wanted His people to know Him, and they weren't getting it through the other means He had tried. He'd sent angels. He'd spoken through prophets. He'd given His instructions to Moses and other leaders to pass on to the people, but it wasn't very effective. So He sent Himself. He became one of us. It would be like you moving to where your cousin lives and learning the language and becoming a citizen of that country! Leaving your life completely behind just to be with her.

Read John 17. This is a prayer Jesus prays to His Father shortly before His death. As you read, write down anything that stands out to you.

What definition of Eternal Life does Jesus give in verse 3?

What does Jesus say in verse 26?

Read John 14:7-10

According to Jesus, is there any difference between Him and the Father (God)?

What does Jesus say in John 10:30?

Jesus was fully human. He was born as a baby. He had human form and a human mind and a human heart. He became one of us. But He was also God. He wasn't an angel or a prophet or a leader anointed by God. He was God. He sent Himself. Why is that important? Well, there are a lot of reasons we won't get into, but one of the most important reasons for us who are living 2000 years after Jesus walked as a human on the face of the earth is this: He still sends Himself.

He doesn't send an angel to deliver messages to you. He doesn't send a prophet to come knocking on your door and tell you which college you're supposed to go to. He doesn't establish leaders who give you a list of rules for right living. He doesn't just send tutors to teach you about Himself, although He often starts there. Ultimately, however, He wants to be your tutor.

Sometimes I wish He would do those other things. An angel suddenly appearing in my living room to give me the latest assignment God has for me would be simpler than spending days or months praying about something and waiting for an answer. But the personal contact with my God is more important than the answer. He wants me to know Him, not just make good decisions.

John 3:16 says, *"For God so loved the world, that He gave His one and only Son, that whoever believes in him shall not perish but have eternal life."* In light of what we have talked about today, what's another way you could say this verse?

Here's my version: "God loved us so much, He sent Himself to show us who He really is. Those who believe and put their trust in Him will know Him personally and intimately, and they will never live apart from Him again. They will continually know His love and depend on it for their very lives."

Is that the way you know Jesus? Do you live and breathe Him? Is He your life? (Write out your thoughts.)

My favorite part of John 17 (Jesus' prayer) is this: *"I have made you known to them and will continue to make you known in order that the love you have for me may be in them, and that I myself may be in them."*

Think of Jesus' prayer this way: It's what He wants for us more than anything. It's His deepest desire for our lives.

He wants you to know Him. And He's never going to stop pursuing you with His presence and His love. Don't look for an angel or listen for prophets. They're not coming. Jesus comes for you. He knocks. Will you open the door? If you do, share whatever is on your heart today: good things, hard things, decisions you're facing, requests…and listen to what He has to say to you.

Delighting In Your God

Delight yourself in the LORD,
and he will give you the desires of your heart.
Psalm 37:4

This is a really cool verse full of a wonderful promise: God will give you the desires of your heart. But what does it mean to 'Delight yourself in the LORD'—the condition of this promise? In simple terms, to delight in something is to enjoy it. Like if you really enjoy ballet dancing, you delight in learning, doing, and watching it. Or if you like reading, you delight in the stories you read. To delight in someone is similar. You delight in your best friend because you enjoy the time you spend together, or you delight in your family because they bring love and joy to your heart that is hard to find elsewhere.

When we delight in God, it means we enjoy Him. We enjoy the relationship we have with Him. We find Him delightful. Is that how you would describe God? Many of us do not see God that way, and this is because we've either been taught things about Him that are not true, or our understanding of Him is limited. You might see God as more of a kill-joy than as delightful. If you do, it isn't because God is really that way but because you're more focused on the things He tells us to do and not do than the reasoning behind it. God has a reason for everything He commands us, and His reasons are always for our benefit. He wants the best for us.

We can delight in our God because He is delightful, but discovering that is one of the great journeys of life. The more you believe God and do what He says, the more you will see His ways really are the best ways. And the more you believe how much He loves you, the more you will believe Him and trust Him when it comes to doing what He says.

What does Psalm 37:4 say God will give us when we delight in Him?

What are some current desires of your heart? (A desire is something you would really like to do or have.)

The second half of this verse is a promise, and it also tells us whether or not we are delighting in God. *'Delight yourself in the LORD and he will give you the desires of your heart.'* This doesn't mean God will give you whatever you want, for often our own wants will lead to destruction and pain (or just what isn't best), and He doesn't want that. He always wants the best for you!

But this does mean that when you are delighting in God, *you will be satisfied.* The deepest desires of your heart will be fulfilled. True satisfaction doesn't come any other way.

That new outfit won't do it. That new phone, or being great at volleyball, or having a boyfriend will all fall short of what you truly need and desire from the depths of your soul. We want to love our God. We want to do the right things and make the right choices. We want to know Him and follow Him. We long to love others as we know we should. And we can! How? By delighting in God.

You may have other desires that are well and good. There's nothing wrong with having good friendships, goals for the future, and fun things to do, but if you're looking to those things to be satisfied, you're not going to find it. Jesus is the only one who can truly satisfy your soul, and if you need any of those other things, He knows that, and He will give them to you at the right time. And knowing Jesus isn't just about having Him as your savior. It's about having a vital, growing, and exciting relationship with Him. One where you believe Him and trust Him with all of your heart with whatever you're facing: a difficult relationship, your schoolwork, peer pressure...etc. You fill in the blank.

How much would you say you are currently enjoying God?

What do you find delightful about Him?

How do you think you can increase your enjoyment of Him?

It's All For You

"...how awesome is the work that I, the LORD, will do for you."
Exodus 34:10

Read Psalm 8:3-5

David is in awe of two things in these verses. What are they?

I hope you didn't choose the moon and the stars as your two things. If you did, go back and look again. Don't miss what David is saying here. David is in awe of God's wonders in the heavens, including the moon and the stars, yes. But this is not all that impresses him.

What he's also in awe of, perhaps even more so, is that God even *thinks of us at all.* 'With all those wonders out there, who are we? Why do You think of us, God? Why do You care?'

What does David say we are crowned with?

Has anyone ever given you something really nice? A beautiful necklace? An expensive gift? Something they made with their own hands? Do you realize God made the heavens for you? He treats us like royalty. Take a moment and think about what that says to you about God's love. Really think about it! Write out your thoughts. (Additional space provided on next page)

Read Exodus 34:1-14

Who are the two involved in this scene?

What does God say about Himself in verses 6-7?

Who is God doing awesome works for? (verse 10)

Read Matthew 27:20-52

How far did God go to show His great love for us?

How powerful was that love (verses 51-52)?

The love Jesus showed to you on the cross was powerful enough to rip heavy cloth, split rocks, and raise the dead from their graves. Now that's powerful strong LOVE! And why did He do it? To raise *us* out of the grave. "Oh, God! Who are we that You are mindful of us? Who are we that You care enough to do so much for us, even give your own life?"

God's response: "You're Mine, and I wanted you to know how much I love you! So stop doubting that."

What are some other ways God has shown you His love? (Think personally and specifically.)

Jesus, thank you for...

—

Always With Me

This I declare of the LORD,
"He alone is my refuge, my place of safety.
He is my God, and I am trusting him!"
Psalm 91:2

When I was young, I went through a difficult time. My best friend and I had a falling-out, and I not only lost a best friend, but she also betrayed me. We were in a combined class of fifth and sixth graders that year, and she became friends with one of the sixth-grade girls in our class who bullied me for the remainder of my fifth grade year. Many of these times took place on the school bus. This girl called me names, threatened to beat me up, and basically made a fool out of me in front of all the other kids on our bus route. I knew Jesus then, and I know He allowed this to happen to me for one specific reason: To show me He knew about it and He cared.

After several weeks of being teased and emotionally traumatized on the bus, I asked my mother to start driving me to school. But my mother taught me a very important truth instead. She said, "Wherever you go, God is with you, and you don't need to be afraid." She had me memorize Joshua 1:9 *"Be strong and courageous...for the LORD your God will be with you."* She told me to pray about it and ask God to help me be strong and courageous. So I did, and the next day a girl I barely knew who always sat near the front of the bus had saved me a seat. And she continued to do so for the remainder of that year!

Read Exodus 33:12-17. What did God ask of Moses? What did Moses ask of God?

What did God promise Moses? (verse 14)

Read Isaiah 43:1-7. What reasons does God give for His promise to remain with His people and protect them? (See verses 1, 3-4)

You are Mine...I am your God...I love you. Let those words penetrate your heart. You belong to God, your Creator and your Savior. You are His, and He loves you.

What are some current situations you are facing where you need to know God is with you and He cares?

Read Isaiah 41:10

Put your name in the blanks below:

> *Do not fear,_____, for I am with you; do not be dismayed, _____, for I am your God. I will strengthen you and help you, _____; I will uphold you,_____, with my righteous right hand.*

Read Psalm 91:1-2

Fill in the blanks with the word *my.*

> *I will say of the LORD, 'He is _____ refuge and _____ fortress,*
> *_____ God in whom I trust.*

Is this true for you? Are you trusting God with your difficult moments?

Remember when we talked about the Kingdom of Heaven? Part of being in God's Kingdom is believing He will take care of you. He loves you, and you are His child. He's not only the King, He's also your Father. You know what that makes you? A princess. You're not just a member of the Kingdom. You're His daughter. And He has promised to always love you and take care of you. How do you think believing that every day could change your life?

What do you hear your Father, the King, saying to you today?

When It Hurts

Jesus wept. John 11:35

"Sticks and stones may break my bones, but words will never hurt me." Ever hear that one? I don't know who first said it, but it's one of the stupidest things I've ever heard. Words hurt. Life hurts. And I don't know about you, but the emotional hurts I've suffered have been way more painful to me than any physical ones, and the pain lasts much longer too.

What do we do when it hurts? When others say mean and hurtful things? When a friend betrays us? When parents get divorced? When the unexpected comes, leaving us feeling alone, confused, and hurting so much we don't know if we can make it through another day?

When "Smile, God loves you!" doesn't cut it? When the encouraging words of others seem so hollow? When that word of criticism goes so deep, you can't shake it? When things don't turn out the way you wish so desperately they would?

I'm going to lead you through some practical steps you can take if you're currently experiencing something painful, or whenever you do in the future. But I'll start by saying, Don't pretend it doesn't hurt. Don't try to deny the pain or block it out. Let it hurt. Cry. Grieve. Be honest with yourself. And most of all, be honest with God. *"Blessed are those who mourn,"* He says. *"They will be comforted."*

List some ways you have been hurt in the past or are currently experiencing emotional pain.

How did (or do) you feel?

Read John 11:1-44

What does verse 35 say?

Why do you think Jesus was crying?

Have you ever seen a grown man cry? Like maybe your dad or grandfather or someone in your church? If you have, it probably affected you differently than when you've seen a friend crying or a woman, such as your mom. Children, teens, and women cry easily, and usually their tears are the result of physical or emotional pain. But when a man cries, it's usually more about brokenness. Something so deep that the willpower to hide the tears is gone.

It seems natural for Jesus to be crying because a friend has died. But in this case I don't think that reason is very logical. Jesus knew what He was going to do. He knew He was going to raise Lazarus from the dead. That's why He stayed away in the first place. He allowed the tragedy so the glory of God could be seen.

So why is He crying? I think His tears are the result of something else going on in this story. They're not about Lazarus' death. They're about Mary and Martha and the rest of the people who had lost faith in Him: He is mourning their unbelief. His friends didn't believe in His ability to bring something good out of a tragic situation. They were angry and blamed Him for their pain.

Have you ever felt like no one believes in you or blames you for their troubles?

Read Hebrews 4:14-16

When we are hurt by others, it puts us in a very weak position. And often we deal with our pain in unhealthy and sinful ways. We may get angry and fight back. We may turn to things to help us escape the pain such as unhealthy eating habits, alcohol, drugs, or sex. We may become bitter toward that person who has hurt us or hate life in general. We may become bitter and angry toward God, shaking our fist at the sky and saying 'How could You let this happen to me?' Or we may simply turn inward and push everyone away, suffering day after day in our own private pain that is never released or dealt with in a healthy, victorious way.

What are some ways you have dealt with your pain? Which ways
have had good and lasting results and which haven't?

Raising Lazarus from the dead was one of Jesus' greatest moments
of His three years of ministry. And it follows one of His weakest
moments. The same is true of His glorious resurrection from the
dead. And that is something we must not miss. We must not miss
it about Jesus, and we must not miss it about our moments of
weakness and difficulty and pain. Take them to Jesus, and let Him
make something amazing and purposeful out of them.

Don't ignore or hide the pain. Don't try to manage it yourself.
Don't shake your fist at God; Run to Him and cry out for help! He
has not caused your pain. He has allowed it for a reason. Go to
Him and find out what it is.

Read James 1:2-4

The end result of difficulty and brokenness that is placed in God's hands is completeness. He is the healer of broken hearts. He is the fulfiller of broken dreams. He is the creator of all things new. He is your God. Go to Him, sweet sister, and weep. He is waiting to comfort you, bring you peace, and give you joy to make it through this and face tomorrow.

Jesus, I really need your help with...

Write Isaiah 41:10 on an index card. Say this verse to yourself.
Review your other verses. What do you hear Jesus saying to you
today?

What Do You Want?

"What do you want?" John 1:38

What do you want? From God? Out of life? It's a good question Jesus is willing to ask you. He was willing to ask His disciples. Read about it in John 1:35-39 and then answer the following questions.

With what name does John identify Jesus? (35-36)

What were these two disciples doing before Jesus spoke to them? (37-38)

What did they ask Him?

How did Jesus respond?

What did they do with the rest of their day?

I believe the entire message of the Bible can be found in this scene. John identifies Jesus, not just by name, but by the title that defines Him best: The Lamb of God: God's greatest display of His love and mercy. Two people follow Him. Jesus sees them and asks them a question, displaying His interest in knowing His people and being known by them. They want to know where He is going to be. He invites them to come and see, and they go—not just for a minute or two, but to stay. It's a beautiful picture of what these men are coming out of—a religion that had been mostly reduced to a bunch of man-made rules, to what God intended for His people from the beginning: A relationship with Him.

In one or two sentences, how would you describe your relationship with God?

Read Revelation 3:14-22

Look again at verse 20. What similarities do you see between Christ's words here and the words He speaks in John 1:39?

Eating is something we do every day, usually several times a day. It's also something we need for survival. Would you say your relationship with Jesus is something you need to survive and also something you enjoy on a daily basis? Are you satisfied with where your relationship with God is, or would you like it to be something more? What do you like about it? How would you like it to be different?

I think this question Jesus asks His future disciples is one of the most important questions He ever asked them. I also believe He wants to ask me and you the same thing. Take some time to think seriously about what your answers are. Be completely open and honest before God right now and write out your response to the first question as if Jesus is sitting right there with you and asking it. Write at least five responses. You can write more. Don't stop until you can't think of anything else to say.

What do you want?

Jesus, I want...

What do you hear Jesus saying to you about these things?

What do you hear Jesus saying about your relationship with Him?

What is your response to Him?

What God Wants

Am I now trying to win the approval of men, or of God?
Galatians 1:10

Do you ever wonder what God wants from you? Do you ever feel you're trying to please a God you can never really please? Do you feel that way about your parents, teachers, or friends too? Write out your thoughts.

Today we are going to be looking at what God wants, and I want you to keep in mind it's not so much about what God wants *from* us, as it is about what He wants *for* us. Remember, God is good, and everything He commands is for our benefit. He wants the best for us! This is not always true of people, and I think that's why we get confused. We think of God as being like our parents or our friends, who aren't perfect. But God is perfect, and that works in our favor—always.

Read Hosea 6:6. What does God say He wants (or desires) in this verse?

I like the way the New Living Translation says it. *"I want you to be merciful; I don't want your sacrifices. I want you to know God; that's more important than burnt offerings."*

The people of Israel at this time were under the Law. They were required to offer sacrifices to God to receive forgiveness from their sins. But it wasn't really about the sacrifices. It was about the condition of their hearts. Making the sacrifices was supposed to get them to think about what they were doing and what was wrong with it. That lying or cheating or stealing or hurting someone had consequences. That living that way wasn't the right way to live. There was a better way.

But many of the people didn't see the sacrifices in that light. They just saw it as a way to escape punishment. 'It's okay if I do this wrong thing because I can just offer a sacrifice and be forgiven later anyway.' Do you ever feel that way? Do you ever do something you know is wrong, all the while thinking, 'It's okay because God will forgive me.'?

Having a relationship with God is about more than being forgiven, it's about *knowing* Him. It's about *trusting* Him. It's about doing the right thing because that's what is best for you. Because that's what will make you happy. Yes, He will forgive you if you mess up, but it's better *for you* to not mess up in the first place. This is who He is, your God who tells you the truth about how to have the best life possible! Why? ...*'Because I'm your God and I love you.'*

Read Galatians 1:10

In what ways are you trying to please others by going against what God says to do?

_____ *Lying to my parents so they won't be mad at me.*

_____ *Lying to my friends so they will like me more.*

_____ *Being mean to someone to gain the approval of a 'better crowd'.*

_____ *Cheating to get better grades.*

_____ *Playing 'dirty' in sports so my team can win.*

_____ *Stealing, smoking, doing drugs, etc... to be cool and impress my friends.*

_____ *Letting my boyfriend do what I know isn't right so I won't lose him.*

_____ *Doing good things, but only to be noticed and praised for my efforts.*

Other...

You know one of the best things about God's Kingdom? There's no ranking system. There's no 'popular' group you have to try and make it into. God doesn't look at your GPA or your stats on the soccer field. He doesn't keep track of how much you go to church or how often you read your Bible; He wants you to do those things so you can know Him better, but He's not 'keeping score' of how devoted you are to Him.

Entering God's Kingdom involves believing God and trusting Him, and that's all you have to do. You're in the door and then you have access to it all. All the blessings, all the love, all the 'approved by God' stickers you could ever want. He just wants you to be there!

Read Matthew 20:20-28

What was the mother's request?

What does Jesus say in the first part of verse 22?

Whom do you think the Father has prepared these "positions of honor" for, as mentioned in verse 23?

I think Jesus is saying, 'It's not about that! It's not about being a super-Christian and Me liking you best. It's about everybody! Everyone knowing Me. Everyone being special! Your sons aren't going to just be near Me, I'm going to be *in* them! *Everyone* who believes and trusts in Me is going to be on My right and on My left. There's enough of Me to go around.'

We don't have to fight for our position in God's kingdom. We don't have to do more good deeds than that other person. We don't have to bring all the right sacrifices. We just have to let ourselves be loved and believe in God's goodness.

Read Matthew 20:29-34

What did these men do to receive their sight?

They asked for it. They had a need and they asked for it. What needs do you have? Take them to Jesus. That's what He wants. He wants you to let Him be your God.

Jesus, I need...

A Picture Of Heaven

"Now the dwelling of God is with men,
and he will live with them." Revelation 21:3

The Book of Revelation, the last book in the Bible, is a very complex and mysterious book. It was written by the Apostle John, the same man who wrote the Gospel of John and three letters we call First, Second, and Third John. This John was also one of Jesus' disciples.

The Book of Revelation is mostly a series of messages and pictures (or visions) that Jesus gave to John, and John simply wrote what he heard and saw. For centuries, scholars and theologians (people who study about God) have been trying to interpret all the messages and visions, and there are many different views of what it all means. I've heard some of those views, and you probably have too. Some I agree with, some I don't, but mostly I feel pretty clueless about it all, to tell you the truth, and I think that's okay because otherwise God would have made Himself more clear.

But one of the things I have seen as I have read this book and gone through various studies on it, is it's not just about future events, but it's about now too. And if we look closely, I think we can see a picture of Heaven in our Hearts through these messages and visions.

Read Revelation 1:1-3

Whom is the revelation about? (verse 1)

What is the purpose of the revelation? (verse 1)

How did God make the revelation known to John? (verse 1)

Who is it written for? (verse 1)

Is it meant to be a blessing or a curse? (verse 3)

Who will be blessed by it? (verse 3)

The second and third chapters of Revelation contain the messages God had for some of the churches active at that time. In each message, Jesus usually pointed out what the people in these churches were doing right, what they were doing wrong, and any rewards or warnings He had for them. In each of the following verses, what rewards are promised?

Revelation 2:7

Revelation 2:10

Revelation 2:17

Revelation 3:4

Revelation 3:12

Revelation 3:20

The common theme in these word-pictures is *life*. Eternal life, which is not just about time, but also quality. A satisfied life. Abundant life. New life. A pure life. A life of security and purpose. And most of all, life with Him!

Read Revelation 21:1-3

Revelation 21 and 22 give us a detailed picture of Heaven. Tomorrow we will look at these chapters. But for now, consider this thought: God is already here, dwelling with us. His Spirit is living within our hearts, and life with Him is not something we have to wait for. We can have it now.

In what ways are you currently experiencing life with God?

Would you like to make God a more active part of your life? If so, tell God that. Write out a prayer asking Him to give you a clearer picture of who He is and the difference He can make in your life right now.

The Throne Of God

At once I was in the Spirit,
and there before me was a throne in heaven
with someone sitting on it. Revelation 4:2

In the movie, *The Prince & Me*, a college student named Paige meets someone on campus who seems to be a regular guy. She believes he is an exchange student from Denmark, but later she learns he is actually the Prince of Denmark who will soon become King because his father is dying.

The Prince doesn't tell her he is a prince. He's tired of everyone treating him differently because he's royalty. He wants to be a regular guy a regular girl falls in love with because of who he is, not because he's a prince.

But the fact she doesn't see him as a prince, doesn't change the fact that he is. He's still a prince who is soon to be King, but she just knows him as Eddie. And I think sometimes we can be that way with God. We have a false impression of Him, and then we make choices based on who we think He is rather than on who He really is.

Read Revelation 4:1-3

In John's vision of Heaven, is the door to Heaven open or closed?

What is the first thing John sees in Heaven?

Read Revelation 22:1-6

Where is the River of Life coming from? (verses 1-2)

What is on each side of the River?

Read John 4:13-14

Who is offering "Water of Life?"

What does Jesus say this Water gives the person who drinks it?

Read Galatians 5:16-23

What is the Fruit of the Spirit? (verses 22-23)

I don't think it's a coincidence that Jesus talks about giving "Living Water", and Paul talks about "The Fruit of the Spirit", and this is the picture of what we see in Heaven in Revelation 22: A River of Life with a Tree of Life on its banks bearing fruit in Heaven.

It's not a huge leap to assume the River provides the water the trees need to grow and flourish. But where does the River begin? At the Throne. Without the Throne, you have no River. And without the River, you have no Tree of Life bearing fruit.

The Kingdom of Heaven is the place where God is reigning and He is on the Throne. If God is not on the Throne of your heart, then that's not His Kingdom. It's yours. Or it's someone else's: whomever you're living for and trying to please.

Look back at Galatians 5:22-23. I think we all want to be this kind of person. And for a lot of years, I tried to be that kind of person, but notice the verse doesn't say, the fruit of *me*; it says the fruit of *the Spirit*.

Jesus in you. That's the secret to bearing fruit that makes you happy and also benefits those around you. That's what makes the water flow. That's the source of love, joy, peace, patience, kindness, goodness, faithfulness, gentleness, and self-control, not your own willpower.

How's your love? Your joy? Your peace? Feeling low on any of these or the other qualities of the Fruit of the Spirit? Lean in close and let me whisper to you, *Jesus is not on the Throne. You are.*

I whisper it because I don't want to have a judgmental tone. I've been on that Throne, and let me tell you, God's Kingdom is way better than my own ever was.

Read Revelation 1:17

What is the first thing Jesus says to John after John sees Him and passes out?

One of our greatest obstacles to putting God on the Throne of our hearts is fear. We're afraid God isn't going to come through for us. We're afraid to trust Him with our everyday lives and difficult circumstances. We would rather take charge ourselves by whatever means necessary. But just because we think we can handle it, doesn't mean we can. And just because we think He can't handle it, doesn't mean He can't. He can! He is able!

Read 1 Peter 5:6-7. Write verse 7 on a note card. How can you personally apply these verses to your life right now?

Good Stuff, Bad Stuff

God saw all that he had made,
and it was very good. Genesis 1:21

To understand the concept of Heaven, it's necessary to go back to the Beginning. Back to when God first created the world and formed human life to live upon it. God created Paradise then, what we commonly refer to as Heaven, and it was not a far-off place or something Adam and Eve had to wait for. It was already there, surrounding them, the moment they took their first breath.

Read Genesis 1:1-2:9

When did God make people? (first, somewhere in the middle, or last.)

Why do you think He made things in that order?

How did man become a living being? (2:7)

What did God think of all He had made? (1:21)

Let this truth sink into your brain: *God is good, and everything He does is good.* Many people don't see God that way, and that is where problems in our thinking of God take root. If we begin with the belief God is only sometimes good, it makes it difficult to trust and understand Him.

Do you think God is good? Why or why not?

If God created everything, and He said it was very good, then where did the bad stuff come from? Why do we have hate, sickness, death, problems, broken relationships...? These things are very real, but they didn't come from God.

Read Genesis 2:15-3:12

The first thing that happened after Adam and Eve disobeyed God was they became ashamed and fearful. Sin is what brings the bad stuff. Not God.

In the next lesson we are going to look more closely at the specific sin Adam and Eve committed and why it had the results it did, but for now take some time to think about your own life. List the good and bad stuff in your life and consider the source of each.

Good stuff:

Who or what is responsible for the good?

Bad stuff:

Who or what is responsible for the bad?

Take some time today to review any verses you have written on index cards. Review previous lessons and refresh your memory of what we have studied so far. How is God speaking to you? What truths are new to you? What does He keep reminding you of?

Believing God

Give thanks to the LORD for he is good;
his love endures forever. Psalm 106:1

Today we are going to take a careful look at the first act of disobedience ever committed by a human being. One thing I'd like you to keep in mind as you read the story and answer the questions is: Adam and Eve were real people. Sometimes it's difficult to imagine that, but they were. And although they were adults in a physical sense, I think emotionally and spiritually they were childlike. Think of Eve as being your age as you read today.

Read Genesis 3

What did the serpent say to Eve first? (3:1)

What was Eve's response? (verses 2-3)

What does the serpent say in verse 4?

What had God told Adam earlier? (2:16-17)

Adam and Eve both knew what God had said. The serpent and Eve were the ones doing the talking, but Adam was there too. Whom did they believe about what would happen if they ate the fruit? God, or the serpent?

Who was telling the truth?

At the root of all disobedience (sin) is a primary problem: WE DO NOT BELIEVE GOD! In this story we know God had told Adam and Eve that eating from the forbidden tree was harmful; but when the serpent said it wasn't harmful and was actually good, Eve believed the serpent instead of God. It wasn't true, but she believed it.

Read Psalm 106:1

What truths about God are stated here?

I asked this before, and I will ask you again: Do you believe this?

If not, what is hindering your belief in a good and loving God?

Believing God: believing He is who He says He is and that He is good and loving is extremely vital to your faith in Him. Faith leads to obedience. Doubt leads to sin. Sometimes God may say things that don't make sense to us. His Word may tell us things that seem too restrictive or impossible to do. But everything He commands is for our benefit. He doesn't make up rules just for the sake of having rules. They have a purpose, and that is where His love and goodness can be seen.

We don't know exactly why the fruit of this tree was bad, but God knew, and that is why He told them not to eat from it. The problem wasn't that God said 'no', the problem was Eve didn't listen. She didn't trust God. She didn't put her faith in the One who told her the truth; she put her faith in someone who lied to her.

Have you ever done this?

What was the result?

Take a moment to think of some things you know God says to do. List them and then write the benefits of living that way. (Additional space on next page)

Example: Loving others. Benefits—It makes me feel good to love. When I love others, they usually love me in return. It brings friendship, joy, and fun times with my family and friends.

Do the same with things you know God says not to do, along with the negative consequences.

Example: Lying. Consequences—It hurts people. It makes me feel bad and trapped in my lies. Others don't always believe me when I'm telling the truth. It creates stress and difficult moments with my family and friends.

If you want to live the way God says to live but you think that is impossible, I guarantee you it's not. Believing God loves you and knowing His commands are for your benefit will go a long way to helping you live obediently.

Write out a prayer to your loving God.

The Tree of Life

On each side of the river stood the tree of life.
Revelation 22:2

Today we will take one more look at Adam and Eve in the Garden of Eden. In the previous lesson we focused on the "bad" tree in the story. It was called the Tree of the Knowledge of Good and Evil, and eating from this tree exposed Adam and Eve to an awareness of evil and brought curses on them. But there was another tree in the garden that had a purpose besides the fruit it provided for eating: The Tree of Life. Let's take a closer look at this tree, and see if we can discover what its purpose may have been and why that matters for our lives today.

Read Genesis 2:8-9

Where in the garden were the Tree of Life and the Tree of the Knowledge of Good and Evil?

Can you think of any reason why God may have placed them there?

Read Genesis 3:22-24

When did the Tree of Life become harmful?

What would have been the harm of eating from the Tree of Life at that point?

What did God do to protect them from it?

We often think of Adam and Eve's banishment from the Garden as their punishment for disobedience, and it partially was, but it was also an act of mercy. God loved them too much to say, 'Okay, now that you have been exposed to both good and evil, you can't eat from that other tree anymore either,' and then left them on their own to be obedient. He knew they would be deceived again (probably by being led to believe eating from the Tree of Life would take away their curses). So instead, He made them leave the Garden and sent an angel to keep them away from the Tree of Life.

Read Revelation 22:1-5

I like to imagine this picture of Heaven, and I believe it is a very real place we will see someday after we leave our lives here on Earth. But I also believe this picture of Heaven contains many symbols of what we can have now.

Jesus calls Himself the "Living Water", so the River of Life may be a symbol of the abundance of Jesus that flows when we are experiencing Heaven in our Hearts. His abundant love and goodness and truth flows into our hearts (right down Main Street, so to speak) touching us and others around us.

The Tree of Life may be a symbol of the cross of Jesus that brings us salvation, or it may also be a symbol of the Truth. The word used for "tree" is also the word used for the type of bark people in ancient times wrote on. So it could be interpreted as 'the writings of life', or 'the truth that leads to life'.

What does Jesus say about "the truth" in John 8:32?

What do you think it means to be set free by the truth?

Jesus came to set us free. He came to show us the truth about who He really is. He isn't a distant, harsh God who doesn't care about us and expects perfection. But rather, He is a loving God who longs to be with us, lead us in the truth, set us free from sin, and help us live within the perfect plans He has for us.

To finish this lesson, write out this sentence at least five times:

God loves me, and He tells me the truth.

She Believed

"Blessed is she who has believed."
Luke 1:45

We've spent the last few lessons looking at the failure of Adam and Eve. To be fair, keep in mind they are not the only ones to ever do so. You and I have done the same, and not just because they messed things up for us. We would have made the same choice they did.

But I would like to look at someone who did believe God during a crucial moment, and what may have led to her belief, rather than her screaming and running the other direction and saying, 'Un-huh, God. I'm not doing that!'

Our main character today is Mary, the mother of Jesus. Read about her in Luke 1:26-45.

What did the angel tell Mary was going to happen to her? (verse 31)

Whom did the angel say this child would be? (verse 32)

What was Mary's response in verse 34?

Have you ever faced a situation that seemed really scary or impossible where you said, 'How can this be happening to me?'

How did the angel tell Mary this impossible thing would happen? (verse 35)

I think when difficult moments come, we need to let Jesus speak the same words to us: 'I'm here. It's okay. My power is overshadowing this. You'll see. Just believe and trust Me.' How could believing those words help you cope with a difficulty you're currently facing?

What does the angel say in verse 37?

What does Mary say in verse 38?

Does Mary's reaction amaze you? It amazes me. In effect she's saying, 'Okay. Whatever you say, God. I'm sure You know what You're doing.' How does her response differ from Eve's in Genesis 3:1-6?

Eve did not believe what God said. Mary did. And while the Bible doesn't say this, I'd like to suggest Mary was in the habit of believing God. Her answer comes too quickly and with too much assurance for her to have never experienced the faithfulness of God before. Read her song in Luke 1:46-55. What did she believe about her God?

How do we see Mary's belief in the ways of God in Luke 1:34?

Mary had embraced her Jewish heritage. Mary likely came from a family where the love and faithfulness of God had been taught to her from her earliest days. She believed in sexual purity before marriage. She knew what was right and what was wrong, and she was living it out in her life.

What does the angel call her in Luke 1:28?

Make no mistake about it. God knew Mary's heart. He favored her because He knew what she would say when this message was delivered to her. He hand-picked her for the part because He knew she would say 'yes'.

How quick are you at saying yes to God? Why do you think that is?

I like what Mary says in verse 49. *"...for the Mighty One has done great things for me."* You may have heard the phrases: 'It's not about me. It's not about you. It's not about us.' They're popular Christian sayings of authors, songwriters, pastors, and others. But they're wrong. It is about us. Jesus makes it about us. He's not sitting up there as the King of His Kingdom, saying, 'Everyone look at Me. See how great I am? Now worship Me because I deserve it!' (He does deserve it, but that's not His Heart.)

His Heart is this: 'I love you. Follow Me because it's what is best for you, I promise. I'm not lying. Trust Me, and it will be okay. Just believe.'

Read Luke 1:45 again. Write it on an index card. How does this verse speak to you today?

River Of Life

"Whoever drinks the water I give will never thirst.
It will become a spring of water welling up to eternal life."
John 4:14

What makes you thirsty? Have you ever been so thirsty you felt like you were going to die if your P.E. teacher didn't let you get a drink of water? Do you remember what if felt like when that cold liquid finally entered your mouth? Today we are going to talk about a different kind of thirst: a spiritual thirst, but it's not that different than needing water to drink every day.

What makes you thirsty? (physically speaking)

What do you like to drink when you're thirsty?

Some things help to quench our thirst better than others, but all of them generally work to some degree. Sometimes we try to live life like that. Our souls are thirsty for things like love and happiness and friendship and to be good at something; and we think we can satisfy that thirst with many different things, but it doesn't work that way. Some things may satisfy for a time, but it usually doesn't last, and then we try something else.

What does Jesus say in John 4:14?

Jesus is talking about a spiritual thirst here. He's talking about being satisfied. And He's saying, 'There are many ways to try to find satisfaction that seem good, but the only thing that's going to last is Me." He wants us to have good things. He wants us to have love and friendships and enjoy our life, but first we need Him. With Him everything becomes meaningful and can bring us joy—even the difficult things. But without Him, everything is meaningless. It might be good or seem fun for awhile, but it won't last.

Read Ecclesiastes 1:1-2

Solomon was a king who had everything. What does he say about life?

What different things did he seek after in the following verses:

Ecclesiastes 1:16

Ecclesiastes 2:1

Ecclesiastes 2:2

Ecclesiastes 2:3

Ecclesiastes 2:4

Ecclesiastes 2:8

What does he conclude about these things in Ecclesiastes 2:10-11?

What does he say in Ecclesiastes 4:4?

Who are you envious of?

How much time do you spend trying to be like that person or impress them?

According to Solomon, will this bring meaning to your life?

What do we never have enough of according to Ecclesiastes 5:10?

What does Psalm 37:4 say?

Remember that verse? Think about how you are trying to find satisfaction and meaning in your life apart from God. What do you need to give up? What do you need to stop trying to get or achieve?

Talk to God about these things.

Fruit Of The Spirit

The fruit of the Spirit is love, joy, peace,
patience, kindness, goodness, faithfulness,
gentleness, and self-control.
Galatians 5:22-23

Begin today by reading Revelation 22:1-5 to refresh your memory of the description of Heaven given in these verses. Then draw a picture of how you imagine it to be. Use colored pencils or crayons if you have some.

I'd like to focus on the Tree of Life once again, but in a different way than before. The Tree of Life may symbolize several different things, and we can't really know for sure, but we do know one thing: It bears fruit.

What is your favorite fruit? Why do you like it?

My favorite fruit is ripe blackberries. I grew up on a farm, and we had loads of them every summer. I like them because they are sweet and juicy. But if they aren't quite ripe, then they're terrible! I think we can be assured the fruit on the Tree of Life is always ripe and perfect for eating.

Read Galatians 5:22-23

How do we get this "fruit"?

If you said from God (or the Spirit), you're right. And we cannot get it any other way. As I mentioned before, one of the common mistakes we make about the Fruit of the Spirit is we try to be loving, joyful, at peace, patient, kind, good, faithful, gentle, and self-controlled on our own. We think this is what God wants from us, and so we try to "measure up" and be the best person we can be.

But it doesn't work that way. It's doesn't say the 'fruit of me', it says the 'fruit of the Spirit'. Only He can bring these qualities out in you. He doesn't want these things *from* you, He wants them *for* you.

Look back at the picture of Heaven in Revelation 22. Where is the Tree of Life?

What kind of water is in the River?

Where can we get that water?

Remember the secret? Jesus in you. Heaven in your heart. Look back at the picture you drew of Heaven. Is your heart a beautiful place like that? Why or why not?

What do you hear Jesus saying to you today?

The Greatest Thing

"Love the Lord your God with all your heart
and with all your soul and with all your mind."
Matthew 22:37

I've talked about the Fruit of the Spirit in this devotional book a few times now, and one reason I have centered in on that verse as we have been talking about 'Heaven in our Hearts' is because I think it's a perfect picture of what it's all about.

"Heaven in my Heart" isn't just a sentimental or poetic phrase. It's a reality that God wants us to experience. It's why He made us. It's why He died for us. It's why He comes to live inside of us. It's how we can enjoy our lives and what will help us through the problems we encounter. It's what can bring us into the Presence of God like nothing else.

Our focus today is loving God. Jesus said the greatest thing we can ever do is to love Him, and the second greatest thing is to love others. Both of these things are a lifetime journey. God's love for us is steady and unchanging. But our love for God and others can grow.

Read Matthew 22:34-40

Who asks Jesus the question, 'Which is the greatest commandment?' (verse 35)

It says this man asked the question to test Jesus. He wanted to know if Jesus knew His stuff. Jesus was considered to be a Rabbi, and Rabbis knew the Old Testament backwards and forwards. In fact, they had it memorized!

I don't know if this particular expert in the law knew the right answer. He probably had an answer in mind, but whether it matched what Jesus said, we don't know. There are a lot of commands given in the Old Testament, and it never says loving God and others is the greatest. Other experts and Rabbis may have thought so too, but Jesus would be the one to know for sure. And whether those who heard Him believed it or not, you and I can believe if Jesus said loving God is the most important thing, then it really is!

Getting back to the Fruit of the Spirit, what is the first fruit listed in Galatians 5:22?

Loving God is not something we can do on our own. We need God's Spirit within us, and as we allow God to reign in our life, the more we will love Him.

But there's another key factor to loving God. It's believing God is worth loving: that He is lovable. What about God do you think makes Him lovable?

Read the following verses. What do they say that makes God worth loving?

Genesis 1:1

Genesis 1:27

Deuteronomy 4:29

Deuteronomy 4:31

Psalm 5:12

Psalm 91:11-14

John 3:16

John 15:9

Romans 8:28

Romans 8:38-39

That was a lot of verses to look up. Thanks for hanging in there. But you know, that's just a little taste of what makes God lovable. I could have listed pages and pages more.

Beyond what the Bible has to say about God, I can also tell you from my personal experience He is worth loving. I've been following Jesus for a long time, sometimes more faithfully than other times, but He has never let me down. He has never disappointed me. There have been times when it seemed like He wasn't there because things weren't going like I planned or wanted, but His faithfulness and reasons for doing what He does always comes shining through.

And that's something you have to experience yourself. One of the ways your love for God will grow the most is to trust Him: to put His love to the test and see what happens. Is He faithful? Does He take care of you? Does He help you? Does He work everything together for good? You won't find out if you don't take the risk of trusting Him.

What is He asking you to trust Him with today?

Loving Others

"Love each other as I have loved you."
John 15:12

Before we get started on a new lesson, I want to ask how you are doing with your independent reading. Have you been reading the Bible on your own a few times a week in addition to doing this devotional book? If you have, that's great, and I hope you are learning to listen to what God is saying to you without any input from others. If you are finding that difficult, keep at it anyway. Be patient as you learn to hear His voice.

If you haven't been doing any independent reading, I encourage you to do that in addition to this study. (The journaling format can be found in the back.) One reason I encourage you in that is because we are more than halfway through this devotional, and when you come to the end, I want you to be in the habit of having that time with Jesus so you won't suddenly be left on your own. I also want to remind you to be writing verses down you find especially meaningful and want to keep fresh in your mind. Review those you have made special note of so far and keep recording new ones. Filling your mind with the truth is one of the best ways to keep moving forward in your spiritual journey.

Now, on with today's reading. Several of these verses would be great to memorize or carry with you wherever you go!

Read John 15:9-17

Whom is Jesus speaking to? (verse 14)

How does He feel about them? (verse 9)

What does He tell them to do in verse 9? verse 12?

Read Matthew 22:27-39

Jesus ties the two commandments together. In both of these instances when He talks about loving God, He also talks about loving others. You can't separate them. If you love God, you will love others. In 1 John 4:7-8, John says, *'Everyone who loves has been born of God and knows God. Whoever does not love does not know God because God is love.'*

So what's the problem? Why do we not always love others as we should? Because we're not loving God like we should. But why? It goes back to what we talked about before. We must find Him to be lovable, and the greatest way we can do that is to fully believe He loves us.

Jesus says this in John 15:12. *"Love each other..."* How? *"...as I have loved you."*

Do you believe He loves you? Has He given you any reason to doubt His love for you? Record your thoughts.

What did Jesus say is the greatest way someone can show their love to someone else? (verse 13)

Did He do that for you? How does that make you feel?

Believing we are loved by God is necessary to loving Him back, and it's also the key to loving others. Why? Because when we believe we are loved by an almighty, loving God who will always care for us even when others don't, then it really doesn't matter how others treat us. We don't love them because they love us. We love them because God loves us. And with God's help, we can love anyone because His love for us is that huge! Believe you are hugely loved, and you will love others hugely too!

Jesus tells us our love for others can be measured by how much we give of ourselves to them. Are you giving in your relationships, or only taking? Are you giving things that matter to others—that truly benefit them? Are you looking out for their interests, or only your own? How could you do this more and with whom?

One of the greatest things about love is it doesn't only benefit the receiver but also the giver. Jesus says believing we are loved and loving Him and others will make our joy complete. Loving others makes us feel good. So if you're feeling bad, maybe you need to take a serious look at yourself. Are you accepting God's love for you? Are you passing that love on to others?

What do you hear Jesus saying to you today?

You're Worth Loving

"Love the Lord your God with all your heart
and with all your soul and with all your mind
and with all your strength...
Love your neighbor as yourself."
Mark 12:30-31

In reading the above verses, you might be saying to yourself, 'Not this again. We've been over this already. I'm supposed to love God, which will lead to me loving others, but I can't do either unless I believe God loves me and He's worth loving.'

Very good. I'm glad you remember all of that. But there is one more part to keeping the greatest commandments that I'd like to share with you today. By the title, you may have guessed it has something to do with you. Specifically that you are worth loving. But we've kind of already been over that. God loves us. For whatever reason, we're worth something to Him. We're extremely valuable and precious to Him. His death on the cross for us proves that, among other things.

But today I don't want to talk about God's love for us, but rather that we must also love ourselves. We must believe we are worth loving. We're special. We're uniquely created by God. We need to care about ourselves, as well as believe God and others care about us.

Read Mark 12:30-31. How many times is the word 'your', or 'yourself', mentioned?

How many times is the word 'God' mentioned?

How many times is the word 'neighbor' mentioned?

I believe God is very specific in what He tells us. I like to do word-studies on the original languages of the Bible because I often find some interesting Hebrew or Greek words that have been translated into English but don't quite say it with the same "zing" as God intended.

And I think this is an example of Jesus speaking very precisely when he uses the word 'your' seven times in the span of two verses and only mentions Himself and others once. Look at the phrasing of verse 30. "Love the Lord *your* God." Do you consider God to be *your* God? Not just your parents' God, or your pastor's God, or my God, but *yours*?

"With all *your* heart, *your* soul, *your* mind, *your* strength." God doesn't expect or want all of us to love Him in the same way. He wants you to love Him in the best way for you. You are His unique creation with unique interests and talents and opportunities. Don't try to love Him the way someone else does. Make it personal for you.

One way I love God is by writing stories and devotional books because it's something He has gifted me to do and I love doing it. It's fun! It makes me happy. It brings me joy. What are some things in your life you would describe that way? Write down what comes to mind on the facing page.

So do them! Have fun. Enjoy your life. Do things that come from your heart and soul. Don't try to put aside the things you love in order to love God. Make Him a part of them. Ask Him to show you how you can do those things better, or to benefit others, or to bring Him glory. And chances are, you can do that best by having a blast with it yourself.

Try new things if you feel Him leading you to, and you'll find you enjoy those things too, even if they seem scary or 'not your thing' at first. And if you try something and really don't enjoy it, stop!

"Love your neighbor..." Who is *your* neighbor? Whom has God placed in your life to love? (Don't assume it's only people who live in a different house than you.)

Some of these people may be easy for you to love, and some may be difficult, but be assured if God wants you to love them, He will give you the ability. He doesn't expect you to love them with your love alone, but with His love flowing through you.

"...as *yourself*." Do you love yourself? Do you like who God has created you to be? Why or why not?

God made you special, sweet sister. Learn to see yourself through His eyes and the eyes of those who love you. Learn to love yourself, and that will go a long way to loving Him and loving others.

List all of the qualities you like about yourself. (How you look, how you act, your talents and interests...)

List the things others have said they like about you, even if you don't see yourself that way.

List the things you don't like about yourself that you can change, and then ask God to help you do that.

Jesus, thank you for...

Jesus, I really need your help with...

What Does Jesus Say?

"The words I have spoken to you
are spirit and they are life." John 6:63

Today we're going to be looking at some things Jesus said about how we should think and act. Let's start, however, by looking at our verse for the day at the top of this page. They are words Jesus spoke. Read them to yourself. What do you think He means?

Read the following verses and sum up what Jesus says in one or two sentences.

Matthew 6:23-34

Matthew 7:1-5

Matthew 7:7-11

Matthew 7:24-27

Which of these speak to you the most today and why?

Read Matthew 12:35. What does this verse say about how we will speak and act?

It's not enough to know what Jesus has said about how we should live. We can know it and not do it. We can want to do what's right and keep failing. Why? Because we try to do things in our own strength and determination.

Jesus doesn't expect us to do that. That's why He came! He came to 'go before us'. To live the perfect life so He can give us strength to do the same. He lives inside of us to give us that power.

Don't try to hide your weaknesses from God. He knows about them anyway. Be honest with Him and ask for His help to live out His life-giving words. *"For everyone who asks, receives!"(Matt. 7:8)*

Jesus, I really need your help with...

He Believes In You

"You of little faith. Why did you doubt?"
Matthew 14:31

Jesus didn't do all of His teaching on hillsides or in the synagogues (Jewish churches). Likewise, He didn't just give talks or preach messages. Many of the things He taught His disciples, He taught them in the midst of their regular lives: While they were fishing. While they were eating. While they were traveling. And while they were in the middle of great crisis.

Today's lesson involves such a time. It's about Peter and something Jesus taught him in a unique and unbelievable way. As you read, try to imagine being Peter.

Read Matthew 14:22-33

Think of a guy (or girl) you know who you would consider to be strong and fearless. Now imagine that person being in Peter's situation. Peter wasn't a wimp or a coward. He was a fisherman, and that was a job for tough men. They weren't just fishing for pleasure like someone on vacation at the lake. This was their job. They worked all night. They had to pull in heavy nets. They often got caught in fierce storms at sea.

How did the men feel when they saw Jesus walking on the water toward them? (verses 25-26)

What does Jesus say to them? (verse 27)

What are some of your fears? List those that come to mind, being as specific as possible.

We live in a scary world. We don't need to be on a stormy sea and see a ghost walking toward us to be scared. There are plenty of scary things to face in our everyday lives right here on land. Crime, tragic accidents, tornadoes, earthquakes, illness. No place is completely safe. Not even our own homes.

And if that isn't enough, we don't only have things to fear such as being physically harmed or being threatened by someone, but we have emotional fears of being rejected by others, not doing well in school, being betrayed by a friend, parents getting divorced or remarried to someone we don't like...the list goes on. If you didn't include these kids of fears in your list above, do so now.

Whatever your fears are, I'd like you to sit quietly with Jesus for a moment and hear Him say these words to you: *"Take courage. I'm here. Don't be afraid."* Write those words across your list of fears.

In this scene with Peter and Jesus, I think we see Peter letting go of his fear, but something else is going on too. He sees Jesus out there on the water, and he decides he needs some kind of proof that it's really Jesus. So he says, *"If it's you, Lord, tell me to come to you on the water."* What a strange thing to say, don't you think? Peter is already afraid, and yet he wants to do something that would be even more scary—get out of the boat! If it was me, I think I would have said, 'Okay, Jesus. I believe it's You. Can you please get in the boat now and calm this storm!'

But Peter doesn't want to wait for Jesus to come to him. He wants to go to Jesus. So Jesus tells him to come, and he gets out of the boat and starts walking on the water toward Jesus. Talk about taking a step of faith! How is he able to do this? First of all, Jesus empowers him to do it, but that's not all. I think Peter also believes he is safe with Jesus.

Do you believe you are safe with Jesus? Why or why not?

At what point does Peter begin to sink?

What did he cry out to Jesus?

What did Jesus do?

What did Jesus say?

When I've read this story in the past, I assumed Peter had lost faith in Jesus, but recently I heard a pastor explain Peter's behavior in a different way. It doesn't make sense that Peter lost faith in Jesus for a couple of reasons. One, he's already walking on water, and he obviously knows Jesus is giving him that ability. Peter's faith in His power would have been at an all-time high. Secondly, Peter trusts Jesus to save him when he begins to sink. He cries out for help. *"Lord, save me!"* he says.

So what's the problem? Peter loses faith in himself. He loses faith in his ability to be doing the impossible. For a moment he is living in the ultimate reality of "Heaven in my Heart". He's doing something that only someone empowered by God can do. But then he looks around, takes his eyes off Jesus, sees the huge waves, and must have thought, 'This is crazy! What am I doing? This is impossible!' And it's then he begins to sink.

"You of little faith," Jesus says. *"Why did you doubt?"* Can you relate to Peter's lack of faith in himself? How so?

Maybe you don't believe you can get better grades. Maybe you don't believe you can overcome temptation and make good choices. Maybe you don't believe you can love that person. Maybe you don't believe you can overcome your fears. Maybe you don't believe you can be happy. Your life is just too hard.

Maybe you don't believe you can experience "Heaven in my Heart". But Jesus believes it. He believes in you. He says, 'Come. Get out of the boat and trust Me to give you whatever you need to do the impossible. Because I will, and together we can do this. You can do it!'

All Things Are Possible

"With man this is impossible,
but with God all things are possible."
Matthew 19:26

In the previous lesson we talked about Peter walking on the water, how he was able to do that, and what made him sink. One key factor I want you to keep in mind: Peter was able to walk on the water because he wanted to and because Jesus wanted him to. Let's look at a couple of other times when people came to Jesus and either got what they were looking for or went away empty-handed.

Read Matthew 20:29-34

I like the way Jesus phrases His question. *"What do you want me to do for you?"* Do you ever feel like God wants a lot of things *from* you but nothing *for* you? If you do, this is wrongful thinking. I was stuck in that kind of thinking about God for a long time, and it kept me from having the kind of relationship with Him that He really desired for me. I felt like I was trying to please a god who was impossible to please, and I was! But that is not my God. That was a false god others had taught me about.

I remember one specific night when I began to realize this. I was going to be speaking at a women's retreat, and I was really stressed-out about it. And the ironic thing was, I was going to be speaking about peace! I had no peace about what I was doing, and when I read these words Jesus speaks, I realized why. My response to Him was, *Jesus, I want you to be pleased with me.* And His response to me was, *Melanie, I'm already pleased with you. You don't have to earn my love. That's not why I'm asking you to do this.*

Do you ever feel like you have to earn God's love? If so, in what ways do you try and do that?

These blind men weren't trying to earn anything from Jesus. They just wanted to see, and they asked Him because they knew He had the power to do it for them.

What do you want Jesus to do for you? Write as many things as you can think of.

Read Matthew 19:16-26

What does this man ask Jesus in verse 16?

Do you see anything wrong with his question?

This was a rich man. I'm sure he was used to getting whatever he wanted. Think about a girl you know who seems to get whatever she wants. If she wants new clothes, her parents buy them for her; if she wants a certain guy for her boyfriend, she gets him; if she wants to be great at something, she is. But let's say she begins to realize something is missing. Something she can't buy. She wants the secret to a truly satisfied heart and she asks someone who seems to have those kinds of answers. 'How do I get that? Please tell me. I'm willing to do anything.' That's pretty much what this man is doing.

Eternal life is not something to be bought or earned. It's something to receive without cost. It's for everyone. When Jesus says, *"If you want to enter life, obey the commandments"*, He's not saying we can earn eternal life by doing good things; He's saying, 'This is what eternal life is: Living the way I have told you to live. Believing in Me. Knowing Me. Trusting Me.' Remember that eternal life is not just about living forever in Heaven, it's also about the quality of life now.

Look at the list of commands Jesus mentions in verses 18-19. Do you think obeying these commands would make a person's life better or worse? Why?

Jesus is basically restating the Ten Commandments here that were given to Moses and God's People we read about in the book of Exodus. (Chapter 20 if you want to look it up.) But He doesn't include all of them, just the second half that can be summed up by saying, *"Love your neighbor as yourself."* So what about the other commands?

1. You shall have no other gods before me.
2. Do not have or worship idols.
3. Do not misuse the name of God.
4. Remember the Sabbath day. Keep it holy.

I think Jesus addresses all of them in His next words. The man says he has kept the commands Jesus mentions. 'What do I still lack?' he asks.

What does Jesus say? (Verse 21)

How do you think this relates to the four commands listed above? (Hint: Money can be an idol.)

This was a good man. He did good things. He may have done a lot of good things with his money to help others. But he wasn't willing to give up all of his money. Why? Because money was a god to him. He was more dependent on his money than on God. On the outside he may have looked like he had everything he could ever want, but he didn't. He may have looked like a good Jew, but he didn't have eternal life. He knew something was missing. And

Jesus tells him, 'You're missing Me. You're missing God for who He really is. You're missing the point.'

Are you happy? Are you satisfied? Are you living the way God says is best for you? If you're not, it's not about 'being good' or earning God's love. It's about knowing, believing, and trusting Him, which *leads to obedience*. Seem impossible? On your own, it is. But what does Jesus say in verse 26? Write out His words.

Look back at your list of what you want Jesus to do for you. Do you believe He can do them? Do you think He wants to?

What do you hear Him saying to you today?

The Greatest Treasure

"...you will have treasure in heaven."
Matthew 19:21

Have you ever gone on a treasure hunt? Did you find anything?
What do you think would be the best treasure you could find?
Money? If you found a thousand dollars what would you do with
it?

Would you go out searching again, or would you be satisfied with
what you already found?

Sometimes life is like a treasure hunt. We're always on the look-out
for that special find: Something to be really good at; A perfect look
that will get a special guy's attention; Figuring out our purpose; A
good friend.

In our previous lesson we read about a man who had all the earthly
treasure he could want. He was rich, and yet he was missing
something. He went searching for it. He went to Jesus and asked
how he could gain eternal life, but he went away empty-handed
because he didn't have enough faith to believe treasure in heaven
was better than what he already had. He wanted it, but not at the
expense of giving up his money.

Is there anything that is priceless to you? Anything you have in your life that you wouldn't give up for all the money in the world? A possession? A really good friendship? Your family? A special talent?

Read Matthew 19:16-24

What do you think Jesus meant by *"You will have treasure in heaven."*?

Read John 14:1-3

In the King James Version of the Bible, verse 2 reads: *"In my Father's house are many mansions."* In the NIV it says, *"In my Father's house are many rooms."* Well, which is it? A mansion is a lot different than a room, right? When I get to Heaven, am I going to be living in a 10,000 square-foot mansion along the Crystal Sea, or am I going to be given a tiny high-rise apartment on Riverside Drive?

Whatever our 'home' looks like in Heaven, I'm sure it's going to be great—more than we could ever imagine. Maybe it will be a huge mansion, or maybe a cozy little cottage, or maybe something much different than the types of homes we're familiar with here on Earth, but I don't think that's what Jesus is talking about here.

The New Testament was translated from Greek, and the wording in this verse is very tricky. The word for "mansions" or "rooms" actually means a place to live or stay, and the word "house"

(Father's house) pretty much means the same thing. In THE MESSAGE, a contemporary language version of the Bible, it says, *"There is plenty of room for you in my Father's home."* I think this is a good wording of this verse because it agrees with the idea that God's love and mercy is for everyone, not just a select few. It's not so much about the size of our 'home' in Heaven, but the fact we have a place in God's Kingdom.

Another possibility for an accurate translation of this verse could be, "My Father dwells in many places." This would fit in with the theme of this devotional book: God wants to dwell inside of our hearts—our 'room' for Him. We don't just go to His House someday, but He has come to us, to dwell where we are. (See also John 14:23)

I believe this is the "treasure" Jesus is referring to when He speaks to the rich man. He's saying, 'You've got all this stuff, but it's meaningless unless you use it for the good of others and put your ultimate trust in Me.'

Read Philippians 3:7-14

Paul's treasure he speaks of is his heritage. He was a pure-blooded Jew from one of the best family-lines. And in that day, that was a big deal. Sort of like if you were the President's daughter, or your mom was the doctor who found a cure for cancer.

But Paul left his prestigious roots to pursue Christ. He says, *'I consider everything a loss compared to the surpassing greatness of knowing Christ Jesus my Lord.'* Knowing Him personally—getting as close to Him as he possibly can. What does he say in verse 14?

What do you think 'the prize' is?

If you said Jesus, you're right. He is our ultimate reward!   What does He say is His reason for coming back for us? *"That you may also be where I am."* (John 14:3) It's not about living forever; it's about living forever with Him! And we don't have to wait for that. We can have it now.

Knowing Him, believing Him, trusting Him: There is nothing better we could do with our lives here on Earth and for all Eternity. Choose to live life with Him now, every day, in every situation, and the greatest treasure you could ever find is yours!

In what ways do you see Jesus as your treasure?

Jesus, you are my treasure because...

Through The Clouds

"In a little while you will see me no more,
and then after a little while you will see me."
John 16:16

Earlier I told you about a difficult time in my childhood when I was treated very poorly by a girl at school. As you may recall, I believe God showed Himself to me through that experience: He knew about it, He cared, and He rescued me.

We all face difficult times, and I know you may have experienced something similar or something more serious, even devastating. Perhaps you are currently suffering through a dark time, or maybe the actual event is well in the past, but the pain, anger, heartbreak, or sadness remains fresh in your mind and heart. You don't need to write down a specific situation, but I'd like you to think about a time like that and how you felt then, or how you currently feel. What different emotions come to mind?

What kind of thoughts did (or do) you have toward God?

I've faced my share of "cloudy times" since I was young that have sometimes placed me on a roller-coaster of faith. One day I could be telling myself, 'It's okay. God is over this. He's got His reasons for this happening. I can trust Him.' But the next I'd be living in doubt and fear again, or screaming 'Why God!'

But no matter what I've been through, I have always witnessed the faithfulness of God. Sometimes it comes quickly, and other times I have to wait, but it comes. I "see" Him come through the clouds.

How about you? Have you "seen" Jesus after a time of darkness?

Read John 16:16

I believe Jesus is talking about a couple of different things here. He says this shortly before His death, the night before He is crucified, and He's talking about that: About dying, being buried, and His friends not seeing Him anymore, and then seeing Him again after He rises from the dead.

I think He's also talking about them not seeing Him after He goes back to Heaven, but then seeing Him again when they die and He "returns" to take them to Heaven, or possibly when they see Him again returning as the Holy Spirit.

Read Acts 1:1-11

How did Jesus ascend into heaven? (verse 9)

How did the men in white say He would return? (verses 10-11)

Read Acts 2:1-4

How did the Holy Spirit come?

Read Revelation 1:12-20

Where does John see "the Son of Man" (Jesus) standing?

The lampstands represent the churches. Here we see a picture of Jesus among His people, not just on the Throne in Heaven. So what does that matter? It means Jesus is already here. If you are waiting to "see" Jesus someday—like when you "get to Heaven", you don't have to wait that long. You can see Him now. He's here. Keep your eyes open and look for Him.

> *"You will seek me and find me when you seek me with all*
> *your heart. I will be found by you," declares the LORD.*
> *Jeremiah 29:13-14*

Read Revelation 1:7

What clouds are surrounding you right now? I challenge you to ask Jesus to break through those clouds. Go ahead. Be bold! Jesus wants you to ask Him for that. He wants you to see Him, but He often waits until you're ready—until you're looking for Him.

It's Yours!

"...for the kingdom of heaven belongs to such as these."
Matthew 19:14

Please read the verses below that are taken from Matthew 19:13-15, and answer the questions that follow.

> *Then little children were brought to Jesus for him to place his hands on them and pray for them. But the disciples rebuked those who brought them.*
> *Jesus said, "Let the children come to me and do not hinder them, for the kingdom of heaven belongs to such as these."*
> *When he had placed his hands on them, he went on from there.*

What are some positive qualities of children?

What are some negative qualities of children?

How do you think the disciples saw these children who were brought to Jesus?

How do you think Jesus saw them?

How are young children different than older children? (A five-year-old compared to someone your age)

How are they the same?

What childhood characteristics would you like to hang on to as you grow older, and which ones would you like to outgrow?

I'd like to point out Jesus doesn't say the Kingdom of Heaven belongs to children, but rather that it belongs to "such as these." The Kingdom of Heaven is for people of all ages, but there are definitely some qualities of children we need to hang on to as we get older in order to experience Kingdom-living. We can "grow up" in the Kingdom, but we must not "outgrow" it.

Read 1 Timothy 4:12

Do you ever feel like people look down on you because of your age? How so?

Do you think you're looked upon better inside of the church, or about the same as anywhere?

In what areas was Timothy encouraged to set a good example?

How do you think you can set a good example for others in the following areas:

Speech:

Life:

Love:

Faith:

Purity:

Look back at your qualities of children. What qualities are necessary to set a good example in these areas?

What negative qualities need to be outgrown?

If there's one quality I believe all children possess more than any other, it's trust. Children are extremely trusting. As babies they are completely dependent on whoever cares for them, and even though they learn to become more independent, they generally remain very trusting of others anyway.

Trusting God is the most crucial element to Kingdom living. It begins with believing He loves you and He is good and everything He tells you is for your benefit. When we believe those things, nothing can keep us from experiencing all He has for us to the fullest measure.

On a scale of one to ten, ten being highest, how would you rate your current level of trust in God? Why?

Read 1 John 3:1

What has the Father lavished on us?

Who are we?

The Kingdom is yours to grab hold of. But your hands have to be free to do so. Free from worry, free from doubt, free from doing things your own way or trying to handle everything yourself. Free to be embraced by Jesus. Allow Him to pull you up onto His lap and hold you close every day. Trust Him to care for you, lead you, teach you, forgive you, help you, and be everything you need Him to be.

In what ways do you need to "Come to Him" now?

The Power Of Love

"My kingdom is not of this world."
John 18:36

You're going to get a history lesson today. If you like history, great. But if you're like me and history isn't your best subject, don't worry, there's not going to be a test. I'm just providing you with some background information to help you understand why Jesus came and the Kingdom He talks about.

You don't have to read far into the Bible to see kingdoms wrestling for power with each other. The story of Noah and the ark he built (where the animals go in two by two) happened very early in human history. What does Genesis 6:11-13 say about what the world was like then and why God sent the Great Flood?

This isn't meant to be a lesson about Noah, but for those of you who aren't familiar with the rest of the story, Noah builds the large ark God tells him to build, and Noah and his family and the animals are saved from a huge flood that covers the whole earth. When the floodwaters receded, only those on board the ark were still alive, and they basically started over again. Noah was a righteous man, meaning he followed God and His ways, and yet not too long after the earth began to become repopulated, people began living in corrupted ways again, and violence became a way of life in everything from family strife to great wars where different people and nations were fighting for their place on the earth.

If you want to read about some of those struggles for power, start reading in Genesis 11, and just keep going. The Old Testament tells about one power-struggle after another, both within families and between nations. But, like I said, that is not our focus today. (This would be a good place to do some independent study if you're looking for someplace new to read.)

By the time Jesus was born, the great Roman Empire had taken over much of what we call modern day Europe and parts of northern Africa, lower Asia, and the Middle East (Israel, Jordan, Lebanon, Syria, and Iraq.) Jesus was born in Israel and lived His life there. Israel had become the Jews' homeland: the Promised Land God had given to His people after Moses delivered them from slavery in Egypt. But their time in Israel was always threatened by surrounding nations as they were involved in many wars, and they were driven out of Israel for a time without returning until many years later.

During the time of Jesus, the Romans were in charge of Israel. They allowed the Jewish people to live there, but they were in control, and most Jews living in Israel at that time were afraid of either being killed by their rulers or being driven away from their homeland once again.

For a long time prophets of God had predicted the coming of a Messiah, someone who would deliver the Israelites from the oppression of their enemies and bring them peace. Jesus claimed to be this Messiah, but the problem was He wasn't a great king or ruler. He was an ordinary man. A carpenter's son from Nazareth.

What does one of Jesus' disciples say about Nazareth in John 1:45-46?

Even His future devoted followers were doubtful Jesus was anything special when they first met Him. Do you ever feel that way? Have you ever asked yourself, "What's so special about Jesus, anyway?"

Jesus was the Messiah as He claimed to be, but He was a different kind of Messiah than the people were expecting. They thought it would be some great ruler who would rescue them and set up His Kingdom in Israel. But what He really came to do was set up His Kingdom in their hearts.

What does Jesus say in John 18:36 about His Kingdom?

What happened to Him after this? (Read John 19)

So, what kind of Kingdom was Jesus talking about? In the next lesson we will talk about that, but for now read John 15:13 and think about God's incredible love for you. A love we see through Jesus when He died to set us free.

Jesus, I know you love me because...

God's Dwelling Place

"Now the dwelling of God is with men,
and he will live with them." Revelation 21:3

Okay, a little more history today, and then we're done. I promise. In the previous lesson we talked about the history of mankind from the time of Noah to the time of Jesus. Review it briefly and write down the major points we talked about.

One part I briefly mentioned I want to look at more closely today is when Moses led God's People away from Egypt where they had been living as slaves under Pharaoh, to the Promised Land of Israel. If you look on a map of this area (you might have one in the back of your Bible), you will see Egypt really isn't that far from Israel. In the U.S., it would be like traveling to the state adjacent to yours, or to the one beyond that, and yet it took them forty years to get there. Why? Mostly because God had some things He wanted to teach them, and also because they didn't trust Him much and had to keep learning the same lessons over and over. He had promised to lead them to a great land where all of their needs would be met and they would be free, but they had to cross the desert to get there. What route did God have them take according to Exodus 13:17-18?

How did He lead them? (Exodus 13:21-22)

In Exodus 14, it tells us before they crossed the Red Sea, Pharaoh changed his mind about letting them go free and he took his army and went after them. God provided a way for the Israelites to cross the Red Sea on a dry path He made for them right through the middle of it, and then when Pharaoh and his army tried to cross in the same place, the waters rushed back, killing all of them and allowing God's People to continue on their journey.

After this, God continued to provide for the people and protected them in many ways, but it was a long journey, and many of them doubted that Moses knew what he was doing, and that the cloud and pillar of fire were really going to lead them to the Promised Land.

It was during this journey God gave Moses the Ten Commandments, which were like blueprints for right living. It was also during this journey God gave Moses instructions to build something. What was it according to Exodus 25:8-9?

Basically this was the first temple, or church, that God told His People to build. But it wasn't a permanent building. It was a huge tent that could be set up when the people stopped in one place to camp, and then it could be taken down and moved until they settled in their next place. What was the main purpose of the tabernacle? (Exodus 25:8)

The rest of Exodus is a detailed description of how the tabernacle was made and all of the things inside of it. This is where God's Presence was, or His Spirit. He wanted to be with His people, but they had to do their part by building a place for Him to dwell. A holy place.

Describe what the people saw from outside the tabernacle or "tent of meeting" when God's Presence dwelt there. (Exodus 40:34-38)

What do you think it would have been like to "see" God in this way?

I think it would have been awesome in a way. To see the glory of God? I can't even imagine that. But I also think it may have made me feel separated from God. I could see Him, but I couldn't go be with Him. I would know He was there, but not have any personal contact with Him.

So, what does all of this have to do with God's Kingdom and the Kingdom Jesus said He came to bring us? The tabernacle, the Jewish synagogues, and the temple in Jerusalem that was eventually built, were all designed as places where God's People could meet with Him. Sacrifices were made there. People were forgiven of their sins. The priests would meet with God directly and then give instructions to the people, but it was all a "detached" way of meeting with God and knowing Him.

When Jesus said, *"My Kingdom is not of this world,"* He meant a new kind of kingdom was needed. Not an earthly kingdom where He would be the king of the land of Israel and allow the people there to live freely for a time and then die like everyone else on the face of the earth anyway, but a kingdom where He would be the king of people's hearts everywhere, for all of time, giving them individual freedom to know Him as their God and have a different kind of peace. Peace in their hearts. Peace as forgiven and loved children of God. Peace that a glorious eternal home would be waiting for them on the other side of death, and peace in knowing everything had a purpose and they could live an abundant, full life, no matter what their circumstances were.

But this was only possible in one way. For God's Presence to not only be *with* them, but *in* them. For His Spirit to dwell in their hearts.

Read John 20

What was the first thing Jesus said to His disciples? (John 20:19)

What did He give to them according to verse 22?

Read Revelation 21:1-7. How do you think this could be a description of your heart with God dwelling there?

Is that what you want?

A Prayerful Heart

"This, then, is how you should pray..."
Matthew 6:9

What comes to mind when you think of prayer? What is prayer?
What is the purpose of it? How often should we pray? Write out
your thoughts.

Prayer is basically communicating with God. Talking to Him.
Sharing your thoughts with Him. Asking Him for things. Thanking
Him. Praising Him. Listening to Him. We do all of that through
prayer. Prayers can be spoken, written, or thought. God can hear
your thoughts, and you can hear His. Prayer can bring you peace
and hope. But it can also lead to frustration if you feel like God isn't
listening or answering. Maybe you've asked God for things you
haven't gotten, and you've said, 'Why bother?'

What does Matthew 6:5-8 say about prayer?

What specific things does Jesus say we should pray for in Matthew 6:9-13?

Of the above, which have you prayed for in the last week?

In Matthew 6:8 it says God knows what we need before we ask Him. So, the purpose of prayer is not to make God aware of our needs. He already knows. The purpose is to realize He is the source of what we need and to go to Him, expecting Him to meet those needs.

Think for a moment about what you really need. Not what you want, but what you need. If you don't know, ask God, and He will tell you. Then, ask Him for those things. (Be sure to include emotional and spiritual needs.)

Look again at Matthew 6:9-13. What beliefs, actions, and attitudes do you think this prayer suggests beyond just saying the words?

Example: 'Our Father in heaven,' isn't just about what we call God, but who we believe He is: our loving Father we can trust.

Beyond communicating with God, I think prayer is also a lifestyle to be lived out in our everyday lives. It doesn't do me any good to pray to my 'Father in Heaven' if I don't see Him that way: If I don't trust Him; If I don't think He's in control; If I don't believe in His authority and power. He wants me to believe it far more than to hear me saying, 'Father.'

Similarly, He wants me to allow His Kingdom to come within my heart, not just ask for it. He's more than happy to answer that prayer, but He can't if I don't cooperate and let Him be in charge. He wants to meet my needs, but I must trust He actually will, not have my own agenda as a back-up plan if He doesn't come through for me.

He will not lead me into temptation, but I can always lead myself just fine. He wants to deliver me from evil, but I must not walk into it of my own free will.

And He will forgive me to the point where my heart is so free and filled with His love I can't possibly hold a grudge against anyone else; but if I don't allow Him to forgive me completely and recognize my need for that, I won't have it to give.

What do you hear your 'Father in Heaven' saying to you today?

A House Of Prayer

"My house will be called a house of prayer."
Matthew 21:13

Start today by reviewing the previous lesson on prayer. What did Jesus have to say about it, and what specific needs did you ask God to meet? Have you seen any answers yet? How has your view of prayer changed?

Read Matthew 21:1-13

What instructions did Jesus give his disciples in verses 2 and 3?

I think there are times when we need to hear God's specific instructions to us. Is there anything going on in your life right now where you feel like you need God to tell you exactly what to do?

Besides you making the right choices and things turning out well, what do you think could be another benefit of you asking for specific instructions? (Hint: Think about how the disciples would have felt after they went into the village and saw the donkey and colt there, just as Jesus had said.)

I believe one of the greatest purposes of prayer is for us to see God more clearly. Asking Him for specific instructions, doing what He says, and seeing things work out will increase our confidence in Him. It will help our faith to grow.

This will also be true if you are continually going to Him with your needs and asking Him to meet those needs. You will see His faithfulness. You will see He's really listening and cares about what happens in your life.

This can even be true if it seems He is not listening. There have been times when I have asked for something I haven't gotten, but in its place God gave me something better—what I really needed, not what I thought I needed.

Briefly explain what happens in Matthew 21:12-13.

Remember the original purpose of the Tabernacle? Exodus 25:8 tells us God wanted the people to build a place for Him to dwell among them. And today as we have God dwelling within our hearts, He has the same purpose for being there. He wants His "House" (your heart) to be a place of prayer. A place where you talk to Him. A place where you ask Him to meet your needs and trust Him to do so.

Is there anything you are striving for on your own, instead of leaving it in God's hands? Is there anything you are looking to others to provide for you instead of looking to God? Think about emotional needs too. Write out your thoughts.

Read Revelation 3:20

Open the door today and let Jesus in. Review the verses you have written. Imagine Jesus speaking the words directly to you. Can you turn any of them into a conversation with Him? What do you want to ask Him for?

Promises, Promises

You will receive a rich welcome into the eternal kingdom
of our Lord and Savior Jesus Christ.
2 Peter 1:11

How good are you at keeping promises? How good are others at keeping promises they've made to you?   When people make promises, sometimes they follow through with them, and sometimes they don't. It's easy to develop a view of God like that: Sometimes He will take care of us, sometimes He won't. Sometimes He will help us, sometimes He won't. Sometimes He will answer our prayers, and sometimes He won't.

Today's lesson is about the promises God has made. Some of His promises are unconditional, meaning no matter what we do or don't do, He will keep His promise to us anyway; Other promises God has made are conditional, meaning if we do our part, then He will do His. Read the following verses and write the promise that is made and the conditions of the promise. (If there are no conditions mentioned, write 'NONE')

Psalm 37:4

Promise:

Conditions:

Proverbs 3:5-6

Promise:

Conditions:

Isaiah 54:10

Promise:

Conditions:

Jeremiah 29:11

Promise:

Conditions:

Jeremiah 29:12-13

Promise:

Conditions:

Matthew 11:28

Promise:

Conditions:

John 14:23

Promise:

Conditions:

John 15:4, 7 (To remain means to stay or dwell)

Promise:

Conditions:

Ephesians 2:4-9

Promise:

Conditions:

Look back at the promises that have conditions. Do you find any of those conditions to be too impossible to keep? Why or why not?

In 2 Peter 1:3 it says, *As we know Jesus better, his divine power gives us everything we need for living a godly life. He has called us to receive his own glory and goodness. And by that same mighty power, he has given us all of his rich and wonderful promises. He has promised that you will escape...and that you will share in his divine nature. (NLT)*

Peter is saying you can be like Jesus. You can love like Jesus. You can avoid sin like Jesus. You can have His goodness oozing out of your heart! And how? By believing in the promises God has made and by getting close to Jesus, which go hand in hand. As you believe God more, you will grow closer to Him, and as you grow closer to God, you will believe Him more.

What promises of God do you need to believe more?

Read 2 Peter 1:10-11

Jesus is waiting to welcome you into His Kingdom every day! He gives you what you need to get there and remain there.

What do you hear Him saying to you today?

Got Love?

And over all these virtues put on love,
which binds them together in perfect unity.
Colossians 3:14

Do you have a favorite outfit? A favorite pair of jeans? Shoes you just had to have? That perfect belt that goes with everything? I bet you didn't know this, but God is into fashion also. He wrote a little wardrobe advice in His Word that applies to everyone, but I think He wrote it especially for us girls. We know the importance of the right color schemes, what looks good and what doesn't, and the perfect accessory to make a favorite outfit complete. If God had His own clothing line, I think He would call it: Got Love?

Read Colossians 3:1-17. What 'fashion advice' for our bodies, minds, and hearts does Paul give in these verses?

1-2:

5:

8-9:

10:

12:

13:

14:

15:

16:

What does verse 14 say about love? Why do you think this is?

Which of these 'fashion accessories' do you need to wear more often?

Some of these things are not easy to do. It's not easy to fix our minds and hearts on Heaven. We are easily distracted by things around us. It's not easy to live a morally pure life in a sex-saturated society. It's not easy to be content with what we have instead of always wanting more. It's not easy to love everybody all the time, especially those who have hurt us. It's not easy to be kind, humble, gentle, and patient. It's not easy to live in peace. No, these things are not easy, but they are vital to living the kind of life God really wants for us, and they are not impossible.

By what names does Paul call those he is writing to in verse 12?

Holy and dearly loved. We don't always see ourselves that way, but God does. Have you ever gotten dressed without bothering to look in the mirror afterwards? Have you ever gotten dressed in what you really want to wear and then put a totally hideous outfit over the top so no one will see the cute one? I doubt it. We want to look our best, don't we?

One thing we need to realize about God's fashion-line, Got Love? is we're already in it. He's given it to us, but often we don't look in the mirror and see who He has clothed us to be. We put our own stuff over the top. Stuff that is totally wrong for us. Stuff that would be better left in the closet, or thrown into the garbage. What are some of those "items" according to verses 5-9?

Holy and dearly loved: you already have that outfit! It already fits you perfectly. You just need to remember you're wearing it and to add the right accessories: tenderness, mercy, kindness, humility, gentleness, patience, and forgiveness. Jesus has given you His Heart. Believing that is the key to walking proudly down that fashion-show runway and strutting your stuff. Believe you are loved, sweet sister. Believe you are forgiven. And God will make you a supermodel of how it's supposed to be.

If you held a mirror up to your heart, what would you see?

What do you think God wants you to see?

Got Joy?

"...so that they may have the full measure
of my joy within them." John 17:13

As you near the end of this devotional, I'm wondering, 'How are you doing? Does any of what I'm saying make sense to you? Is it making a difference in your life?' I hope it is, and that may be clear to you, or maybe you're not sure. For me, "Heaven in my Heart" is something that is easy to live out at times, and then at other times seems completely elusive and impossible.

One reason for that is because we can't always see what God is doing. Sometimes because we aren't looking; We're too distracted by other things and we get our focus off of Jesus. But other times we're doing fine, but God chooses to blindfold us. Things are going on we can't see or understand, and that can make us feel lost and confused, like we're not doing something right, or we messed up somewhere along the way and we can't find our way back to where we were. But don't always assume that because things get confusing or seem totally messed up that something is wrong. You might be exactly where God wants you to be and doing exactly what He wants you to do. But how can you know? That's what this lesson is about. Even when you can't see the truth, you can know it.

What do the following verses have to say about joy?

Nehemiah 8:10

Psalm 16:11

Psalm 89:14-16 (Rejoicing is a form of joy)

Psalm 126

John 15:9-11

1 Peter 1:8

Knowing God will bring us joy. Our circumstances may not be joyful, but we can be joyful. Joyful doesn't always mean happy and pain-free. It's about hope. Hope in believing better days are coming. Hope in knowing we are safe in God's love and His truth will not change. The joy of knowing Him is our strength because we know He is always faithful and good. We can count on that. Even if we make mistakes and take the wrong path at times, He can still rescue us with His grace.

In John 15, Jesus ties joy in with believing in God's love for us and obeying Him because we know His commands are for our benefit. And in John 17, Jesus says He came to bring us the truth, to tell us what we need to know so we can have a full measure of joy.

How do you think knowing the truth and having joy are connected?

Think about a time when you knew a good secret. Maybe it was a time you knew about a surprise birthday party for someone, or you knew what someone was getting for Christmas before they did, or you knew a certain guy liked your best friend before she knew it. You had joy because you knew the truth, right? But the other person didn't have that joy yet because they didn't know the truth.

God's love for us is like that. It's the secret that can make the most difficult circumstances bearable. It's the secret that can bring us joy when it doesn't seem to belong. And the best part is, it's not a secret! God has told us plainly, 'I LOVE YOU!' And it's in that love we can find joy. We just have to remember the truth when everything around us seems to be telling us something else.

How's your joy? Are you believing in God's love for you? Are you believing your difficult circumstances have a purpose—a good purpose for your life?

Jesus, thank you for...

Jesus, I really need your help with...

Got Peace?

And the peace of God will guard your hearts and your minds.
Philippians 4:7

In the previous lesson we talked about joy. We talked about the source of joy being a belief in God's love for us. And we talked about joy being an indicator of how much of His love we are receiving.

Well, guess what? Peace comes in pretty much the same way. Peace and joy are closely related, and generally speaking, I think when you have joy, you will have peace, and when you have peace, you will have joy.

In the following verses, what is the source of peace?

Isaiah 48:18

John 14:27

Philippians 4:6-7

There are two primary obstacles to peace. One is disobedience. When we are not living the way we know is right, we will not have peace. And the second is fear. We are afraid of what might happen. We are afraid God will not take care of us. We are worried about ourselves or someone else.

The remedy for both of these is trust. We must trust His way really is the best way. We must trust what God says, and we must choose to live rightly, believing He can help us to do so.

We must also trust that when we are living rightly, God will take care of us. When He tells us not to be worried or anxious, we really do not have to live that way. We can live in peace.

What are some unpeaceful situations you are facing?

Do you need to make any changes in your choices and behavior regarding these things?

What do you need to believe about God in order to have peace?

How do you think God's love for you, your love for others, joy, and peace are related?

Read Ephesians 3:14-19

This is my prayer for you, sweet sister. Embrace His love for you and go in peace.

What do you hear Jesus saying to you today?

Live Loved

Therefore as God's chosen people,
holy and dearly loved...Colossians 3:12

I hope you have enjoyed this devotional book, and I hope it has given you a better understanding of who God is and who you are as His child. His holy and dearly loved daughter. His princess. He is your Father. Your perfectly loving, always right Father. He is your King. He is your Love. No one will ever love you more than God. And God will never love you any more or any less than He does right now. There is nothing you can do to lose it or gain it. But you can lose sight of it.

This happened to me, and that is why I wrote this devotional book. I've known Jesus since my earliest days, and the first thing I was ever taught about Him was He loved me, and I believed it. In my tiny four-year-old heart, I believed it, and although there were times I doubted or lost sight of it as a young child and as a teenager, most of the time I believed it, and it shaped who I was. I grew up as a loving, forgiving, gracious person. I wasn't what I would call popular at my school, but I had a lot of friends. They liked me because I treated them well. Because I was a loving person. Because I had Jesus inside of me, and I knew it. I knew I was loved, and for the most part I lived like it.

I'm not sure exactly when that began to change. I don't think it was any one time, person, or church that got me thinking differently, but somehow I lost sight of God's love for me. Not fully. I continued to go to church, and I was involved in ministry. I read my Bible, and I prayed, but something was missing. I could feel it, but I didn't know what it was.

There came a time when it was so bad, I felt like I couldn't breathe most days. I became very fearful, confused, and angry at life and God. There were some things going on in my life that were hard, and I mainly saw those problems as the cause of the way I was feeling, but once those issues were resolved and I knew I should feel better, I didn't. I felt lost and alone.

One day I was listening to a Bible-study leader speak, and she said something about going through a difficult time in her life where she made a lot of mistakes, and how she knew part of the problem was she didn't believe God loved her. And it hit me: *'I'm not believing God loves me anymore! I'm trying to do all this stuff to earn His love. I'm not trusting Him with these problems. I don't believe He cares about me enough to help me and protect me. I don't believe He is good and always wants what is best for me. I'm living as His slave, not His beloved child.'*

In some ways it's been a long journey to get back to where I was in believing in His love for me. But in other ways it happened overnight. I chose to believe I was loved completely and unconditionally by my God and to live like it: To "live loved". I began to read my Bible differently, filtering everything through this truth: God loves me. And if what I was learning or had been taught wasn't matching up with that truth, I no longer accepted it as the way I should be thinking.

Read Romans 12:1-2

What 'view' does Paul tell us we should have? (verse 1)

What kind of 'sacrifice' are we supposed to give?

How does he say we will be transformed? (verse 2)

What will be the result?

I like the way these verses are translated in THE MESSAGE: *So here's what I want you to do, God helping you: Take your everyday ordinary life—your sleeping, eating, going to work, and walking-around life—and place it before God as an offering. Embracing what God does for you is the best thing you can do for him...Fix your attention on God. You'll be changed from the inside-out...God brings the best out in you, develops a well-formed maturity in you.*

I hope you fully believe in God's love for you. I hope you know it's not something you have to earn. If you do, don't ever let go of that. No matter what anyone else tells you about what you should be 'doing for God' or how attractive other ways of life may seem, don't get down from His lap and away from His loving arms because you think you don't deserve to be there, or because you're reaching for other things. Remain in Him. Remain in His love, and you will find perfect rest and happiness there.

But if you're realizing you're not there—that you're not living as a holy and dearly loved child of God, then the climb up to His secure embrace is not far. He's reaching out His hand to help you up. All it takes is a step forward, a hand out, and you whispering to Him, 'I believe'.

Live loved, sweet sister, because you are. Live loved and you will become more loving. Live forgiven and you will become more forgiving. Live holy, as one He died to set free, and you will make better choices. Live loved and you will find what I have found: There's no better way to live.

Journaling Format

Date_____

Today I read_____

What does it say?

What does this mean in my own words?

How can this specifically apply to my life?

What changes do I need to make because of what it says?

How can this be an encouragement to me?

What do I hear God saying to me?

What is my response to Him?

*I'd love to hear how God has used
this devotional-study to touch your heart.*

Write me at:

living_loved@yahoo.com

Made in the USA
Lexington, KY
10 October 2018